# FAIRY TALES
## Dreams
### and
# Reality...

**Where are you on your path?**

Copy Editor and Interior Design: Constance Santego

Cover Design: Jennifer Louie

Ordering Information:

Quantity sales. Special discounts are available on quantity purchases by corporations, associations, and others. For details, contact the "Special Sales Department" at the address above.

Trade paperback ISBN: 978-1-990062-15-5

eBook ISBN 978-1-7772220-2-4

Created and published In Canada. Printed and bound in the United States of America

Published by Maximillian Enterprises

Kelowna, BC Canada

www.constancesantego.ca

ALSO BY DR. CONSTANCE SANTEGO

**FICTION**
**The Nine Spiritual Gifts Series:** *(based on actual events)*
Journey of a Soul – (Vol 1 Michael)
Language of a Soul – (Vol 2 Gabriel)
Prophecy of a Soul – (Vol 3 Bath Kol)
Healing of a Soul – (Vol 4 Raphael)
Miracles of a Soul – (Vol 5 Hamied)
Knowledge of a Soul – (Vol 6 Raziel)


**NONFICTION**
The Intuitive Life, The Gift of Prophecy, Third Edition
Fairy Tales, Dreams and Reality… Where Are You On Your Path? Second Edition
Your Persona… The Mask You Wear
Angelic Lifestyle, A Vibrant Lifestyle
Angelic Lifestyle 42-Day Energy Cleanse
Archangel Michael's Soul Retrieval Guide
Tesla and the Future of Energy Medicine
Scaling Beyond 6 Figures: *Strategies for Health & Wellness Professionals*
Beyond the Mind: *Harnessing the Power of Astral Projection for Creative Awakening*
Bend, Don't Break: *Finding Your Way Back to Abundance*
*SECRETS OF A HEALER, SERIES:*
Magic Of Aromatherapy (Vol I)
Magic Of Reflexology (Vol II)
Magic Of The Gifts (Vol III)
Magic Of Muscle Testing (Vol IV)
Magic Of Iridology (Vol V)
Magic Of Massage (Vol VI)
Magic Of Hypnotherapy (Vol VII)
Magic Of Reiki (Vol VIII)
Magic Of Advanced Aromatherapy (Vol IX)
Magic Of Esthetics (Vol X)


**ADULT COLORING JOURNALS**

*SERIES - ZEN COLORING:*
Quantum Energy and Mindful Living Journal (Vol 1)
Reiki Energy Journal (Vol 2)
Nine Spiritual Gifts Journal (Vol 3)
I Forgive Journal (Vol 4)
*SERIES – COLORING PROSPERITY:*
Genie-Inspired Mandalas and Wealth Journal (Vol 1)
Entrepreneurial Mindset Reboot (Vol 2)


**FOR CHILDREN**

I am Big Tonight. I Don't Need the Light!


**COOKBOOK**
My Favorite Recipes, with a Hint of Giggle


Fairy Tales, Dreams and Reality...

# FAIRY TALES
## Dreams
### and
# Reality...
#### Where are you on your path?

For the person who is on a quest of understanding themselves and who enjoys the ease of becoming that person they always knew they were...

# Dr. Constance Santego

Maximillian Enterprises Inc.

# DEDICATION

I would like to dedicate this book to my mother.
For without her I would not be here.
But honestly, without her I would not be the woman I am!
Love you, Mom!!!!!

# TABLE OF CONTENTS

**Acknowledgements** ~ ~ ~ ~ ~ ~ ~ ~ ~ ~ ~ ~ ~ ~ ~ 1

**Prologue** ~ ~ ~ ~ ~ ~ ~ ~ ~ ~ ~ ~ ~ ~ ~ ~ ~ ~ 3

**Introduction** ~ ~ ~ ~ ~ ~ ~ ~ ~ ~ ~ ~ ~ ~ ~ ~ ~ ~~9

**Fairy Tales** –

Enticing your mind for more knowledge ~ ~~ ~ ~ ~ ~ ~ ~~ 12

Once upon a time ~ ~ ~ ~ ~ ~ ~ ~ ~ ~ ~ ~ ~ ~ ~~~~ 13

Old Shoe ~ ~ ~ ~ ~ ~ ~ ~ ~ ~ ~ ~ ~ ~ ~ ~ ~ ~~22

Swan ~ ~ ~ ~ ~ ~ ~ ~ ~ ~ ~ ~ ~ ~ ~ ~ ~~ ~ ~ 26

Castle ~ ~ ~ ~ ~ ~ ~ ~ ~ ~ ~ ~ ~ ~ ~ ~ ~~~ ~ ~ 30

The Maze ~ ~ ~ ~ ~ ~ ~ ~ ~ ~ ~ ~ ~ ~ ~ ~ ~ 34

**Dreams** – *Creating your reality* ~ ~ ~ ~ ~ ~ ~ ~ ~ 40

Dreams, Wishes and Desires ~ ~ ~ ~ ~ ~ ~ ~ ~~ ~ ~ 41

Achieving your Dreams ~ ~ ~ ~ ~ ~ ~ ~ ~ ~~ ~ ~ ~~ 46

~ Manifestation ~ ~ ~ ~ ~ ~ ~ ~ ~ ~ ~ ~ ~ 49

~ 100 goals ~ ~ ~ ~ ~ ~ ~ ~ ~ ~ ~ ~ ~ ~ ~51

~ To attract your perfect mate ~ ~ ~ ~ ~ ~ ~ ~ ~52

Ways to improve your Health,

Wealth and Happiness~ ~ ~ ~ ~ ~ ~ ~ ~ ~ ~ ~~ ~ ~ ~56

~ Health ~ ~ ~ ~ ~ ~ ~ ~ ~ ~ ~ ~ ~ ~ ~ ~57

~ Wealth ~ ~ ~ ~ ~ ~ ~ ~ ~ ~ ~ ~ ~ ~ ~ ~60

~ Happiness~ ~ ~ ~ ~ ~ ~ ~ ~ ~ ~ ~ ~ ~ ~ 64

~ Muscle Testing ~ ~ ~ ~ ~ ~ ~ ~ ~ ~ ~ ~ ~65

~ Things that make us laugh ~ ~ ~ ~ ~ ~ ~ ~ ~ 66

# TABLE OF CONTENTS

**Reality**

Scientific stuff that you might actually enjoy reading ~ ~ ~ 66

Reality - Fact/truth ~ ~ ~ ~ ~ ~ ~ ~ ~ ~ ~ ~ ~ ~ ~ ~ 67

What influences us to make our decisions/paths in life? ~ 71

Understanding the control you have in your reality ~ ~ ~ ~ 73

Maslow's hierarchy of needs ~ ~ ~ ~ ~ ~ ~ ~ ~ ~ ~ 74

Body versus Mind ~ ~ ~ ~ ~ ~ ~ ~ ~ ~ ~ ~ ~ ~ ~ ~ ~ 77

Let's explore how the body and mind are connected ~ ~ ~ 78

Central Nervous System ~ ~ ~ ~ ~ ~ ~ ~ ~ ~ ~ ~ ~ ~ ~ 79

Peripheral Nervous System~ ~ ~ ~ ~ ~ ~ ~ ~ ~ ~ ~ ~ ~ 81

Memory – Limbic System ~ ~ ~ ~ ~ ~ ~ ~ ~ ~ ~ ~ ~ 83

Types of Memory~ ~ ~ ~ ~ ~ ~ ~ ~ ~ ~ ~ ~ ~ ~ ~ ~ 85

The Mind: Conscious, subconscious, and superconscious~ ~ 88

Amazing how fast life can change ~ ~ ~ ~ ~ ~ ~ ~ ~ ~ 89

Stress ~ ~ ~ ~ ~ ~ ~ ~ ~ ~ ~ ~ ~ ~ ~ ~ ~ ~ ~ ~ ~ ~ 93

Holmes and Rabe Social Readjustment Rating Scale ~ ~ ~ 97

Healing Stress ~ ~ ~ ~ ~ ~ ~ ~ ~ ~ ~ ~ ~ ~ ~ ~ ~ ~ 98

      Social Expectations

      Etiquette ~ ~ ~ ~ ~ ~ ~ ~ ~ ~ ~~~~~~~~~ 103

      Manners ~ ~ ~ ~ ~ ~ ~ ~ ~ ~ ~ ~ ~ ~ ~ 104

      Change~ ~ ~ ~ ~ ~ ~ ~ ~ ~ ~ ~ ~ ~ ~ 113

Conclusion – putting it into practice ~ ~ ~ ~ ~ ~ ~ ~ 116

**Appendices –**

**Bibliography**~ ~ ~ ~ ~ ~ ~ ~ ~ ~ ~ ~ ~~~~~~~~~~ 118

**Epilogue** ~ ~ ~ ~ ~ ~ ~ ~ ~ ~ ~ ~ ~ ~ ~ ~ ~ ~ ~ 119

Fairy Tales, Dreams and Reality...

# ACKNOWLEDGEMENTS

I would like to thank my husband for the journey we
have taken together.

My children for being the wonderful people they
have grown into.

My many students and acquaintances have helped me
develop my belief system.

Jennifer Louie, my long-time friend, for being able to understand
my concept and draw the front cover for me. Master Carver Tony
Randazzo, thank you for carving me this wonderful rendition of the
Old Lady's Shoe.

And all the people who helped me edit
and create this book:

| | |
|---|---|
| Diane Bayuz | Kim Hooper |
| Bev Gretzinger | Lynn Hooper |
| Linda Henry | Jennifer Louie |

Fairy Tales, Dreams and Reality...

My little sister and me…
Let the Dreaming begin.

Fairy Tales, Dreams and Reality...

# PROLOGUE

I believe I do luck out in life.

My path seems to be that I can have a good time without drugs and alcohol. I do not need a kick start to my imagination or pretend I am having fun. I really am.

I think I had a pretty typical upbringing. I had many life lessons just like most other kids.

I was conceived in Kelowna, British Columbia, Canada, but for who knows what reason, I was born in Prince George, and two years later, we moved back to Kelowna, where my younger sister was born. We moved about nineteen different times by the time I was eight. At the age of eight, I remember my *first major path change*…my mom left my dad.

We moved to Lloydminster, Alberta.

I did not get to grow up with toys or entertainment like handheld video games (they had not been invented yet), let alone being allowed to play in the house with my friends. So, I played outside, always in earshot of my name, calling me home or a whistle for the same reason. *Thank God my mom used to whistle and not yell out my name… CONNIE… to get me to come home (how embarrassing that would have been).*

I remember this one cold winter day; my two guy friends and I had jumped over the back fence, running to hide in a big water pipe that crossed under a road on the neighboring farmer's acreage. The pipe was big enough to crawl into and sit comfortably on the ice. As the three of us sat there, it was kind of funky; we were out of the wind, and it was so quiet. One of the boys pulled out a cigarette and said, "You should not smoke it, though, because it is not healthy for you." Of course, I said, "If you two are, then I am." So, I had my first few puffs of a cigarette. I didn't know I had to inhale, so I didn't. It wasn't too bad. I don't remember smoking again until I was fourteen.

This next time was very different; my girlfriends wanted me to smoke because they wanted to and said, "I wasn't cool if I didn't." And this time, I did inhale…*YUK…*

*Are you people crazy… what fun is this? I can still recall the gross taste of the smoke going down my throat… choke, choke, choke…* as you can probably guess, I do not smoke to this day.

Coffee that was fun too…Mom used to tell my sister and me that if we were going to drink coffee or tea, it had to be black because the sugar and cream would make us fat. I tried tea once when I was about ten and didn't like it much. When I felt all grown up (about the age of fifteen), I decided to have my first cup of coffee. I had gone shopping and stopped at my favorite little trendy lunch spot…McDonalds…I ordered my black coffee and lunch, sat down and took a drink…well, what a surprise. Again Yuk, Yuk, Yuk. *I have since been told that McDonald's has changed their coffee to a very good-tasting brand many years later. I don't think anybody's black coffee would have positively affected me.*

A few months later, I was in Europe for two weeks on a school trip, and after a few days of drinking only orange juice, since water bottles were not popular or maybe they had not been invented yet, I needed something else to drink. So, I tried tea with lots and lots of sugar and cream. It wasn't too bad. By the time I arrived back home, I was drinking it black. Even owning a café, I still cannot drink coffee and barely drink tea.

Beer…now that is another wow…try fourteen with a girlfriend and three guys parked in a dark area away from anyone…we had seven warm beers each within about two hours. Of course, we were trying to be cool in front of the guys; they were from another school and a couple of years older. All I remember is feeling that everything was in slow motion, and when I got home, all I remember is the toilet and me puking…No, I do not drink beer to this day…the thought or smell of it still makes me almost gag.

Marijuana…okay, yes, I tried it when I was sixteen. The first two times, nothing happened, really nothing at all. But the third time…now that was another story. I was going to another cousin's wedding with my cousin and her boyfriend. It was after the ceremony, and we were driving around before the reception. My cousin's boyfriend lit up a joint, so I asked to try his joint even though my cousin didn't want any. By the time we did get to the reception, all I remember is seeing in tunnel vision and about as far ahead as my hand could reach out at the buffet table and my Great Aunt (the bride's mom) coming over and telling them to get me out of there NOW. I guess I looked like I was stoned, or maybe I was acting weird, that I do not remember. All I remember was that I didn't get to eat… No; I have never done any type of recreational drugs again.

Fun? I am unsure if pretending to be all grown up is worth running down that path.

Fairy Tales, Dreams and Reality…

However, I do feel that I am lucky on my chosen path. What if I did get used to all those things like I did tea… Do I miss all that type of fun…not in the least! Do I pay a price for barely drinking alcohol, doing drugs, or even drinking coffee…? Ya a little…I do not get called out to be with friends as much as I did. It seems I am not the mirror they want to see. A mirror is a metaphor for something/someone that reflects an image that might remind them that they drink and smoke, and I guess maybe the feeling is guilt, responsibility, or shame when I am around.

Do I remember what I did, said, or felt the next day when I go out?

Yes, and I have no regrets about what I did the night before or whom I did it with. My children do not know what I am like with a hangover…sleeping past, driving them to school, or anywhere else they want to go to. I never had to get mad because they were too noisy; my head hurt from the previous night's binge. Their food was always prepared because my stomach was not queasy. The bills were paid on time because I didn't spend the money on those other path choices.

No… friendship and family are a price I am willing to pay for a trade of not having to go through all those so-called fun 'alcohol or drugs.'

My **second major path change** was when I was thirty-one. Shortly after selling my first company, I worked for the man who bought my company, and he let me go a couple of weeks into it (they didn't say if it was red). I was an industrial seamstress working in the back of the shop with my stepsister and the rest of the staff. A few days before, I had told the foreman that I didn't think the one guy would last long because he knew too much, meaning he was too smart, and in this field of business, the smart ones own a company. A few days later, he left. A couple of days after that, my stepsister gave notice of leaving (she went to work for her uncle), but he thought I was to blame for both people leaving…crazy how life goes. They thought I had talked them into leaving. I should have just kept my mouth quiet and not told the foreman anything. By the way, a few months later, the guy opened a business as a competitor.

The stress of not having a job and signing a contract saying that I could not open another sewing business anywhere in BC for the next five years was a very depressing path. Thank God I decided to change my path, and within a year, I had gone for more education and opened my own business in the natural health field.

My **third major path change** was when I was forty-one. My son would move out and go to university in Vancouver, yes…

Fairy Tales, Dreams and Reality...

*I had empty nest syndrome even though he had not even left yet.*

I decided to follow one of my big dreams. I had always dreamt of living in a castle, so my husband, daughter, and I moved our college to the Princeton Castle Resort in Princeton, BC. (You would think that was the path change, but no).

For five months before we moved into the castle, we were there every weekend renovating (it was only a two-and-half-hour drive from Kelowna). By September, we were living at the castle. A couple of months later, my path changed…

We had just put our house up for sale in Kelowna, and the very next day, my husband freaked out, took it off the market, and decided to move back to Kelowna that weekend. He missed the money he made and the life we had there. Hearing that her dad was moving back, our daughter moved back even faster the next day. She missed all her friends and was able to graduate with them.

Great, did I love the path I was on? *No*…both of them were going home, and I still had two months left of teaching the group of students at the castle and could not leave.

I had a hard time making myself happy with the decision to move back to Kelowna…I loved the castle property…but I also loved being with my husband…after twenty years of marriage, I still wanted to be with him.

While I was living alone at the castle, Hubby was figuring out his world at home and whether he could move to the castle permanently. I experienced living alone during the week and seeing him on weekends. It wasn't easy *(again, I hated that path of living separate lives!!!).*

For years, my role was to get the children off to school, work from 8:00am to 5:00pm Monday – Friday and part day on Saturday, make dinner when I got home for the four of us, tidy the house, talk about our day, watch a little TV or sometimes play a game, on weekends we would do yard work, renovate our house, clean the house, go to dinner and/or a movie. In my spare time, I would write my book or read a book, balance our books, sew belly dance outfits for the class I was taking, do glass art, or take a bath, all before nine o'clock at night…oh how I love my sleep.

…the four of us did lots together…the two of us did even more together…I invited my husband to almost everything I did...he did the same. We did do a few things by ourselves…He has his sports that I do not like to play…with vision in only my right eye. Some sports are just not much fun. He does not like taking glass art classes, writing classes, or belly dancing.

Fairy Tales, Dreams and Reality...

My life's path was about to change again, and I knew I could not have what I was going to have at the castle back in Kelowna or vice versa.

The difference was while living alone at the castle, I could still do most of what I did, but I did not have someone to talk to when I wanted to…not true; I could call on the phone and talk…but I could not feel them near me…

I am sure this feeling of being apart is similar to empty nest syndrome or when a loved one dies…they are not there for you to touch and feel. It feels very different when you do not seem to have a connection with them…

**Pleasure and pain**…The castle was my pleasure, but his pain. I was going to move back for him. He was so much happier in Kelowna than at the castle…I would move back for love… Weeks after moving back to Kelowna, he said that he had made a mistake, and when everything was just right, he would return to the castle. The soonest would be in six months.

**The** problem was I was scared that it would never be right and that there would always be an excuse for him not to return. And I would get used to living by myself, and so would he…and worse yet, that we liked it.

Yes, I did move back to Kelowna. Money started to play a role in the decision; it was getting tight with the costs of paying for three homes in different places (Our son was at university).

The pain I felt of hubby being away was bad, but adding the pain of having no money to it made the path even worse.

Because of my path choices, *from my own doing or due to others,* I know that I love to have a man in my life…someone I can love and be with…my best friend. Someone I can do things with…talk to…hold…love…I love the challenge of owning my own business and having some (even if it is imaginary) control of my financial destiny.

*Pleasure and Pain… Why do you choose the path you are on?*

I touched one of my Dreams.
*How are you doing?*

# INTRODUCTION

# Fairy Tales, Dreams, and Reality...

If all the path experiences in your life were awful, you might have grown up with these sayings:

*"What doesn't kill me makes me stronger."*

*"Adversity (difficult or unpleasant) builds character."*

*"Desperation creates innovation!"*

**I have been helping people change their path for years** through my seminars, courses, private or group sessions, and the books and course manuals I have written. This book will guide you through various styles of interpretation of path choice and techniques to change your path.

This book is for those of you or your loved ones who are on a path that is not liked and do dream of a better future, wishing for a change in everything in life or just a little bit of change. I am bringing science, new age, dreams, and fairy tales together for you to understand, test out, and, if you like the new information…to change your reality and path forever.

Here is a toast: I lift my glass…may each and every day be better than the previous…for all of us to have a new opportunity to change our path to a better one!!!

***Success is not a destination or, as Miley Cyrus sings,***

***'It's the Climb'!***

# Fairy Tales, Dreams and Reality...

## Where are you on your path?

*Second Edition*

# FAIRY TALES

**In every culture, storytelling** is a medium used to entertain, educate, instill moral values, and preserve cultures passed on from generation to generation.

## Once upon a time . . .
*(Sorry, this does not have the elements of a real fairytale, but it is still a story and worth reading)*

Fairy Tales, Dreams and Reality...

# Not so long ago . . .

*A* cold brisk wind was coming in from the north, even though it was only October, you could feel winter was on its way.

Kay Thompson's hood was drawn far over her head almost covering her eyes. She had pulled the robe she was wearing around herself even tighter, trying not to let the cold breeze get near her thin body.

It had seemed like days since she last had something to eat and weeks since she had a bath. *What was I thinking? I must be mad trying to find happiness. Well, that is what I thought the man had said that I would find happiness. I am almost ...*

Days before she had taken a seminar on personal uplifting and financial improvement. The motivational class was to get a person pumped up and ready to improve your life.

As she was listening to the speaker, a couple behind her kept talking to each other. *Don't they think of anyone else but themselves?*

It was really starting to bother her. They were being so rude.

She shrugged her shoulders a couple of times wishing they would get the message.

Finally, they shut up.

Now she could concentrate on the speaker.

He was a middle-aged man with dark hair and a mustache, nicely dressed in a casual way. Standing in the center of a large platform that was a few feet above the seats so all could see him better.

He had a great voice and the talent to speak to the audience with clarity and motivation. His words made you feel like you "could" change your life and do better for yourself.

As he talked, Kay started to think about her life and how she really needed a change. *I hate being who I am. I don't like the way I look anymore, maybe never did, but hate it even more now. I just turned forty and life was supposed to be great. Kids all grown up and almost gone. Nice house, great job and have all the toys, boat, RV, etc. We had gone on many wonderful family trips. What could be missing?*

Suddenly, Kay popped out of her daydream. She had drifted off for a few minutes.

Fairy Tales, Dreams and Reality...

The couple behind her had started to talk again.

The speaker was still talking about getting your life back and how you had stopped living the life you were meant to live.

"Remember when you were kids" he said, "And life was exciting and fun?"

He continued to speak. "A child's world is very small, usually a few feet around him or her. A child notices people or objects that are immediately in his path or very, very close. A baby's world is even smaller, just a few inches around the baby. As we age our space gets bigger and we start to notice and care about our car space, house space, desk space, town or city space, province, state, or country space, one day it may even be our planet space."

Kay started to think about her chair space and how she wished it didn't include the two talking behind her.

The two were talking about how people could have their own space, even if they were beside another person and how sometimes you want someone in your space and how other times there are people you don't want anywhere near your space.

Their conversation and the speakers were both starting to get Kay.

The speaker was now talking about controlling your space.

Kay was getting so mad she couldn't hear anybody anymore. *How could I control any of my space? I can't even control my thoughts, which now want to kill the two behind me because they cannot shut up and let me concentrate on what the speaker is saying.*

She started to drift off again into her own thoughts of yesterday.

She just got home from work and as she entered the house you could hear both of her teenage children's music blaring from each of their rooms.

After putting her things down, she walked into the kitchen and started to make dinner, same old thing, meat, potatoes, and veggies.

After a long day's work Kay was always so hungry…and never had the energy to make something special or different.

While the food was cooking Kay opened the mail to find to her surprise—*not*—more bills to pay.

Seeing the bills triggered her to more thoughts, *how does anyone afford to live now-a-days? My husband, John, has always made good money working. We could always afford shelter, a nice place to live, food on the table, and clothes on our backs. I personally do the best I can but with owning my own business one never knows when the money will be coming in.*

As the kids grew up, Kay and John were able to afford to let them try out new sports and entertainment.

Both had their favorite fun.

Jack, her youngest son, was fifteen, and was into music, and Kevin, her oldest son, was seventeen and into video games.

As they grew from babies and until the two had stopped growing, VV Boutique—Value Village—was a great store to buy their clothes from. *They grew so fast, who could keep up?* Designer what? Not in this family, especially back then and with what, good looks and buttons?

Kay's thought changed to a memory of driving by a beautiful home with little kids playing outside.

*How do they do it? How do the families live in such beautiful homes and with kids that are much younger than mine?" John makes much better than minimum wage. We do own a nice car and truck. Sure, we paid full price and have high loans. At least it is a write off through the company.*

It is what she keeps saying to herself to feel better.

*I deserve to drive a nice car, I work hard. I so often don't take home a wage so in my mind it is justified. I know one day I will make good money and I do love owning my own business.*

Again, Kay thoughts snapped back to the seminar as people in the room started to laugh.

She looked around to see what had happened. The speaker had made a funny comment, and everyone was laughing at what he said.

She heard him ask his assistants to pass out paper and a pen to each person.

Next, he had everyone move into groups of four or five from the row of seats they were sitting in.

Once in the group the task was to quickly discuss the group's thoughts on what makes people happy and to write the words down on the piece of paper.

Kay joined the group in her row and smiled and said, "Hi".

One of the guys in the group took the initiative and started by saying "Family and grandchildren make me happy."

Others started to say what made them happy. 'Money, gambling, swimming, hiking, love making, seeing a baby animal start to walk, running, drinking was even one, and the list went on…'

Then the speaker had everyone write down what makes them sad.

Kay's group said things like, 'Sad movies, loved ones dying, bad food, not feeling adequate, our looks, no money, war, loss of a cherished item, accidents, incurable disease, and a few more things…'

Next the speaker said, "How would you make your life better…to mean something? Write down one way you can improve your life."

Some people in Kay's group said, 'Give everyone a hug, notice one beautiful thing daily, help someone in need, bite your tongue, smile, yoga, Tai chi, live, love, laugh.'

As everyone at the seminar sat back in their original seats, the speaker came to his close. He finished by saying, "Take what you learned from tonight and make every day a great day, even if you are not feeling up to it. Make sure you smile a little more, laugh even when it might not be really funny, put a skip into your step and start becoming the person of your dreams."

Kay thought to herself, *did I miss that part…Dreams? Did I drift off when he was talking about that part?*

The two behind Kay started to talk again as they were getting up to leave the seminar.

Kay quickly turned to look at them as she was also getting ready to leave and wondered how they slept at night?

Then Kay remembered what the speaker had said about young children, how they only notice things very close to them.

Well, Kay and everyone around the two behind her obviously were not close enough and the two of them must be immature if they cannot keep quiet while someone else is talking.

Kay drove home daydreaming, imagining what life would be like when…

*When what? When I have a beautiful home, more money, nicer trips… when…I want, I want, I want…*

Kay suddenly remembered a book she read a long time ago. *What did it say? If all you do is think about wanting something, then that is what you are going to create, attract to you…wanting. And you will keep attracting situations that make you want things. You will never really achieve the item, just the wanting of it will be achieved.*

Fairy Tales, Dreams and Reality...

*Pick your words carefully, she thought to herself.*

*Pick your words carefully.*

Kay remembered the speaker from the seminar saying, "Be careful what you think, you just might get it".

She remembered some other books she had read. One talked about what you think you create. And another author wrote about "focus" being your destination, just like driving a car. If you start to look left, you will most likely start to drive to the left.

Kay had been to so many motivational seminars and had listened to many great speakers.

She remembered one, who stated, "*Act it and it will become!*" and another, "Dress for success!"

Kay's main thought was, *Man, they make it seem so easy. So, what is the secret to a happy path?*

She started thinking further back to the question that she had asked her parents, aunts and uncles of how they made their money and to her surprise no one could really tell her.

One of her kin said, "Luck and lots of hard work and more luck." One said, "It was different back then. Lower house prices, food, gas, etc. and wages then were not much different to now."

Another said, "We didn't need all the extravagance you kids need today."

Kay thought to herself of how easy for them to say that when they are the ones that let her, and her cousins experience that kind of life they were used to before they went out on their own. Then expected the kids to be able to create the same life even when necessities went up in price and wages didn't.

*The level of life they have is high but seems so enjoyable. Maybe it is just me... Do I really need all that stuff, house, and holiday home, car, toys, trips, entertainment? Maybe the golden days were better...you went to work from dust to dawn, came home, read out of the Bible (if you knew how to read) and went to bed. They had no TV, movies, computer, or video games...all they did was work, eat and be merry. Yah right, not in this lifetime.*

Kay really was not happy with her life, and she seemed to watch other people get what she wanted, wished and desired.

Kay made it home safely from the seminar and went straight to her bedroom, lied down on the bed and started to cry.

Fairy Tales, Dreams and Reality...

After what seemed like many minutes of crying, she took her driver's license, bank card, and medical card, then went and told John she was going for a walk.

She walked to the nearest neighborhood pub and had a drink, or two or maybe it was three…but who's counting?

After an hour or so she walked to the nearest bank and took out $500.00 cash out of their savings account.

*Saving for what? A rainy day… well I need a better life. John and the kids will be better off without me holding them back.*

Kay walked to the bus station and bought a ticket for the next bus, which was going to Vancouver.

She was thinking to herself, *who cared really where it was going.*

She had friends there that she could stay with. Maybe if she had not been buzzed from the drinks, she had earlier she would not have made such a rash decision and hopped on the bus.

Kay picked up a brochure left on one of the seats as she got off the bus in Vancouver.

It was advertising a retreat in the mountains. She took it as a sign from God and paid a taxi driver to drive her to the address on the brochure.

$200 later.

*Oh well… it is just money. Who needs it anyway, it does not buy happiness…right?*

The brochure read:

Trying to find

- Yourself, oneness
- Calm, peace
- Awakening
- Inner beauty
- Enlightenment

To awaken the real person inside of you • All that you can be, then you are going to the right place!!!

Kay finished paying the driver and walked into the office of the retreat, which happened to be a Buddhist monastery.

The monks were all bald; women and men, wearing red robes and they bowed when greeting you.

After registering, Kay followed the monk who waved at her and said, "This way to happiness."

Fairy Tales, Dreams and Reality...

She was shown into a room with a shower and was given a robe and sandals.

All her belongings, which consisted of; shirt, jeans, underwear, the three cards she took as identification, and the remaining money, approximately $280.00 were all taken from her.

The monk said it would be stored for her and showed Kay where to sit down.

As she sat down, another monk with a razor came toward her.

*What was I thinking...my hair? Well, I went this far, it is only hair, and it will grow back.*

A few tears came as she saw her hair fall onto the floor.

After the Monk was finished, Kay was guided to the shower and was told to wash and remove all her makeup. To dress and come into the main hall.

*I think I lost my mind, no hair, red robe, and sandals. I am sure there must be a better way... but...I just left my husband, children, and life. What was in those drinks I had? Why did I drink in the first place? ...oh ya, I remember, to find happiness?*

Following many monks in the same red colour robes, Kay walked slowly down the big hall.

She entered a room with massive double arched hand carved wood doors and was instantly in awe, it was the most beautiful room she had ever seen.

Facing her, from across the room, was a twenty-foot tall and almost as wide golden Buddha in a sitting position. It reminded her of the little one she remembered polishing at her grandmother house. She loved to rub its belly for luck when she was helping her grandmother dust her ornaments.

Everything in the room was so pristine and clean; red walls with intricate designs in gold, flickering glowing candles everywhere and to her amazement were rows of many itty-bitty wooden benches.

Kay immediately found out by watching the others that you lift the little bench up, kneel and sit on the wood, which has a slight angle for a seat.

Kay knelt with her legs under her like all the other monks and found to her surprise the bench was very comfy and supported her bottom end very well as she waited.

She was not told what to do next. So, Kay waited and looked around at the other people wondering what they were doing.

It did not take long for her to figure out what to do since she had been sober now for quite awhile.

All the other monks were meditating or praying, and she was meant to do the same.

It had been a while since she was last in any kind of church.

*Again, what was I thinking…what am I doing here. What am I supposed to do now?*

A few dragged out hours had gone by and Kay was not used to sitting still for that long in meditation, her legs were beginning to cramp.

Luckily, just as she thought she would have to stand up due to the pain, the monks in front of her started to stand up and leave.

She followed the same waving monk as she had when she come in.

He showed her to her room and said, "Supper will be announced shortly."

Once in the room, she shut the door and sat on the small cot and began to cry.

Thinking about what she had done—leaving her husband and children behind and was now bald with a very shiny white head.

In that moment, she decided to get up and run out of the monastery.

She had no need to sneak out because no one was around to notice she had left.

She ran down the road that the taxi had brought her up on.

She had not noticed how far the vehicle had driven to get to the retreat.

No matter, she kept on running, then slowing down to a quick walk.

Looking back quickly over her shoulder as if someone would come after her.

It seemed as if the early night sky had turned into the pitch of black— as if someone had turned a light switch from on to off.

Kay started to get cold and pulled the hood up and over her head.

In her haste, she had forgotten that she had left all her clothes and belongings behind.

*Well, I am not going to go back for them now.*

All she could think now was, *almost home, I am almost home, I am…*

Fairy Tales, Dreams and Reality…

Suddenly, Kay woke up and realized that she was in her own bed and that it was just a crazy dream.

But just to make sure, she got up and touched her head. and looked into the mirror.

Only to find that her hair was just as beautiful as it was before.

*The End*

Most of us have had crazy dreams, and some of us have even lived them in real life, but it is never too late to change the path that you are leading if you do not like it!

Really, why would anyone take their life path this far? It would seem to me that it would be much easier to just learn how to change your path to a good one. *How, you ask?* By using the newest paradigm.

Which is: *'What you think is what you create'*…

This is the newest paradigm in our time. The books and documentaries, The Secret by Rhonda Byrne or Law of Attraction by Esther and Jerry Hicks or What the Bleep Do We Know or Masaru Emoto's water crystal experiments are all teaching this newest paradigm.

*'What you think is what you create'*…

There have been many other beliefs and scientific paradigms that people have believed differently than the norm.

So again…*What you think is what you create!*

* A Paradigm is an idea or theory different from the norm and is eventually proven as a fact. An example of a famous paradigm is the belief that the Earth was round and not flat as believed. Galileo Galilei believed and tried to prove that the Earth was round and not flat. The authorities of that era arrested him and put him in jail, and after many years, he died… in jail. All because of his difference and passion for this new concept.

***"The Ragged Shoe"***

*Representing a worn-down house:*
*if you can even call it a house.*

*People who are living in conditions that are*
*not even to their own standards.*

**Take a good look at the picture of the OLD SHOE …**

Do you remember the nursery rhyme?

> The old woman who lived in a shoe?
>
> There was an old woman
>
> Who lived in a shoe?
>
> She had so many children
>
> She didn't know what to do
>
> She gave them some broth
>
> Without any bread
>
> And whipped them all soundly
>
> And sent them to bed.

**One belief of the meaning of this nursery rhyme is:**

Origins of the Rhyme "There was an old woman" in Regency England? At first glance, the words "There was an old woman" would appear to be nonsense, but it is believed to have origins in English history! There are two choices of origin! The first relates to Queen Caroline (There was an old woman), the wife of King George II, who had eight children. The second version refers to King George, who began the men's fashion of wearing white powdered wigs. He was consequently referred to as the old woman! The children were the members of parliament, and the bed was the Houses of Parliament - even today, the term 'whip' is used in the English Parliament to describe a member of Parliament who is asked to ensure that all members 'toe the party line.' As a point of historical interest, the wigs worn by women of the period were so large and unhygienic that it became necessary to include mousetraps in their construction!

http://www.rhymes.org.uk/there_was_an_old_woman.htm

**My interpretation is:**

*A ragged shoe-*
  Representing a worn-down house: if you can even call it a house. People living in conditions that are not even to their standards.

*An old lady who lived in the shoe-*
  A frustrated person who cannot make ends meet.

*So many children-*
  So much responsibility and without any resources.

*Gave them broth and no bread-*

Fairy Tales, Dreams and Reality...

Gave them something but not what was dreamt, wished, or desired.
*Whipped them soundly-*
Shut them up.
*Sent themto bed-*
Got them out of the way.

How many of us live (or lived) in places that we had to, not desire to? Ate what was there just because there was no extra money for fancy foods? Wore last year's last year's clothes because the kids came first? Worked at a job because that was all we could find?

Your first few years of life seem to determine much of your path. Depending on how you were brought up and what belief system you had will guide you along your path.

*"My parents were the ages of 16 and 19 when they had me, and I remember as a very young child the four of us, including my younger sister, living in a one-bedroom basement suite, as at first, that was all they could afford.*

*My father had grown up very much like this nursery rhyme; too many people living in very cramped quarters and with a very strict mother. I was told once by my dad's cousin that my grandmother used to whip my dad, and once it hit his ear and made him bleed.*

*Dad had four much older siblings, and when he was eight, his father died on a fishing trip. My grandmother did receive a small CN railroad pension from the death of my grandfather, and since she had no other training and had to support the remaining children still living at home, she had to take in boarders to help pay the bills.*

*Frustrated, I am sure, my dad was very young with no post-secondary education and now on his own with the responsibility of raising his own family.*

*My mother was also brought up in a larger family with five other siblings. She did not finish high school but did continue her education by taking bookkeeping courses through Herbert's Business College and two years towards her Registered Industrial Accountant (RIA) by correspondence and night courses, but the difference was her role models; she still had both parents, and they owned their own business.*

*Funny how life goes... my father treated us the same as he was treated: spankings and being yelled at. He used to buy us frivolous stuff that we could not afford, like fancy cars, too many animals, or toys, because that is what he thought was a good husband and parent. My mother also treated us like she was raised: clean, fed, and well-treated.*

Fairy Tales, Dreams and Reality...

*My mother finally left him when I was eight (coincidentally the same age as my dad was when my grandfather died). She moved to another city where her family (my aunt and uncle) helped her get back on her feet by giving her a job and a place to live.*

*They both left the marriage and went their own way; after all these years, my mom is a self-made millionaire, and my father has gone to court for child molestation. Obviously, they decided to take very different paths."*

Our personal beliefs are set in motion by our parents' beliefs. We follow their religion, eating habits, holidays, what they will pay for and take us to for entertainment, and house rules such as bedtimes, curfews, and chores. Who we can play with, how often, what we wear, what our hair cuts will be, and so forth. It is not until about the age of twelve that most of us have any choice of our own rules. By sixteen, we may have added a few more choices, depending on our parents' beliefs, and right up to leaving home and being on our own, and then many of us are still run by our parents' looks, words, or dollars.

We are influenced by what we really liked or really disliked (positive or negative influences) growing up and who we received compliments, praise, or discipline from parents, grandparents, aunts, uncles, teachers, prayer groups, friends, and the friend's parents, even acquaintances, TV, books, and the internet.

*I also find it interesting how siblings can be brought up in the same way, from the same parents, but end up walking very different paths. It seems evident on my mom's side of the family tree that all the children in each family have led very different lives from each other.*

**So, how will you change your path and boot on your own terms?**

**"The Ugly Duckling"**

*We all try so hard to fit in; how we look, our jobs, house,
car, etc., and we forget to just be ourselves and become the
beautiful person we were born to be.*

Fairy Tales, Dreams and Reality...

**Look at the SWAN in the picture.**

As in the story of the **Ugly Duckling:**

The story goes that a mother duck was sitting on her eggs when the eggs all started to hatch. She noticed she had one very different, funny-looking duckling compared to all the others. As the days went on, it became very ugly, grew very large in size, and did not even walk or swim like its brothers and sisters. Its siblings would tease him immensely for his differences. The ugly duckling always felt different and sad that it never fit in and looked or acted like the other baby ducks. As time passed, he kept growing bigger and bigger, so very different from the rest of his family, making him feel sad.

While swimming in the pond one beautiful afternoon, he saw some new visiting birds swimming there and noticed that his reflection in the water resembled these new friends. That day, he found out that somehow his egg was mixed up, and he was not a duck but was considered one of the most beautiful birds in the world…a white swan. From that day on, he lived happily ever after as a white swan everyone admired.

**I believe** we all try so hard to fit in; how we look, our jobs, house, car, etc., and we forget just to be ourselves and become the beautiful person we were born to be.

I find that one of our biggest mistakes today is we still judge.

*Years ago, when my kids were small, I noticed my son did not naturally do what my daughter did. I found this very interesting because they are only eleven months apart. Other than how they dressed; I treated them much the same.*

*Unlike my daughter, my son wouldn't just naturally help around the house. I would have to beg and plead to have him help me. Then I noticed my son would help his dad without much complaining.*

*My husband grew up with a stay-at-home Mom and three other siblings. He didn't have to do too much around the house. He mostly took out the garbage and mowed the lawn.*

*I talked long with my husband, explaining that our son was copying him. I asked if he would change and help more around the house to show our son that it was also a guy thing to do.*

*Wow! It worked. From then on, my husband had to change to help our son progress and develop into a fine young man.*

Fairy Tales, Dreams and Reality...

*Another lesson I learned about judgment was when my son was about seven and was very tall for his age. One day, we were in line at the cashier to pay for the products we wanted to purchase at a store, and he asked me what a sign read. The sign had really easy words that any English grade two student should have known. I had a couple of weird looks from some other people who were standing in line. I told him (a bit loud) what it said and then continued to say that he would be just as good as the English-reading kids in the next couple of years. Both our kids were in French Immersion and had not fully learned to read English like other English-speaking children. I was told they would balance out by grade ten. Most second-language students excel in both languages in secondary school, which he did, and he now enjoys studying Japanese and Spanish.*

*I have had a few personal experiences where people judged me.*

*One of my biggest was owning an industrial sewing, manufacturing, and repair business when I was twenty-five. An older gentleman came in looking for the boss man. I said, "Okay," walked out into the other room, came back, and said, "How can I help?" (I know that wasn't very nice). I was so tired of people judging my knowledge just because I was young, and this one, to boot, thought I had to be male. He didn't walk out, but the look on his face was definitely one of shock. Once I started to talk, he knew I knew my stuff. I had worked in my parents' business since I was twelve and knew what I was doing.*

*With the same business, I owned a small car, a four-year-old white Sprint, which I had bought brand new and had parked out front in the same spot for years. It was paid off in full. My husband and I decided to trade the Sprint for a used two-year-old red convertible Pontiac Sunbird. We now had a $17,000.00 loan.*

*In the first few weeks of owning the car, many regular clients said, "Wow, nice car. Business must be doing really well. I could not believe it... I now had a big payment... but I must be doing well.*

*A few years later, I decided to move the business. My mom and I shared some space, and she found a location for half the price and only two hundred square feet smaller. So, we moved. This new location was closer to the town center but a little hidden, and there was great parking front and back. It was one story, skinny and long, whereas the original place was two floors, wide and short, with terrible parking.*

*When we moved, my regular clientele kept asking what had happened. Were we okay?*

Fairy Tales, Dreams and Reality...

*Crazy, now that we looked smaller from the front, we must be doing worse. I lost some business because of the move. I have found over the years that people, in general, only judge from their perspective: visually (what they see), auditory (hear), thoughts (think), or feelings (feel). We need only to gauge, not judge. It is okay to look at someone so that you can decide on how to change yourself or how you do not want to. This means I look at people I admire and those I would never want to be like to improve my life. I have often wondered how someone has become successful and made enough money to buy a fancy house, car, etc., so I can expand my perspective on other ways to better myself. If I do not find a way to educate myself, how can I change? So, I educate myself by watching, listening, trying, and do not forget dreaming...*

I get crazy looks from my family and friends when I tell them my big dreams! Thank goodness my husband usually wants similar things, so he does not judge me too much. But I cannot help but notice how his family and mine judge me. At family get-togethers, they ask me what is new, and when I tell them many times, I catch them rolling their eyes in disbelief or shaking their head. It is hard to hold on to your dreams when your loved ones do not have faith in them ever coming true. But do not fret too much. There are many ways to take control of your life… meaning you decide instead of life deciding for you. You will find it easier than you think to take the first step... and change your beliefs on your path to that fairytale ending.

**"The Castle"**

*Owning a castle... just for make believers?*
*Dare to dream big.*

Fairy Tales, Dreams and Reality...

**Take a look at the CASTLE in the picture.**

A castle, have I lost my mind…

What… Connie owns a castle… that is just for make-believe.

For years, I dreamt of living in a castle… I know, most little girls do. I remember telling my husband about us living in a big fancy house (with turrets and pillars and such).

He would tell me to dream on.

I remember first telling my students that my dream was to live in a castle. I was terrified of the remarks I was going to receive. I said it very shyly and quietly.

But eventually, I said it with confidence… and low and behold one day, when I told the class to dream big and that my dream was to live in a castle, one of the students piped up and said she lived at a castle…and it was for sale.

I asked her where she lived. I have had many students from all over the world, and I wondered where she came from.

She answered that she lived in Princeton. I asked her if she meant Princeton, BC, two hours away Princeton. She said "yes" and showed me the castle online at the break.

My husband, the student, and I visited the castle that weekend. Sure enough, she did live there; her family looked after the property then.

Even though it was freezing in January and the snow was past my knees, I fell in love with the place. It even had a hundred-and-fifty-seat amphitheater.

By February, I had met the owner, and we got along beautifully. I decided to move the school to Princeton and live at the castle. In April, we signed the lease and started the renovations. There were many to be done. By September, we had moved to Princeton and were ready for our next program intake.

I loved it!!!!!!!!! You enter the castle with a big driveway circling the property, statues everywhere, a huge fountain, and a moat with a drawbridge.

We were going to open a restaurant and do retreats in the summer.

But my family did not love it as I did! As stated in the prologue.

Do you know how many nights I cried?

Many, I could not believe that my fairytale dream was ending so fast.

Fairy Tales, Dreams and Reality...

So, how are you going to change your path and keep it? No matter what, we really do choose our path, and I do believe we have the option to change it if we do not like it... I will own a castle again one day. I can feel it... I just do not know when! One way to change your path is by dreaming...and letting your mind wander. The other is to be careful what you ask for. Whatever you do, do not let go of your dreams.

**"The Path"**

All of us, every day, have a chance to change our path
to a better one each and every day.

**Take a look at the PATH in the picture.**

Notice how it changes. We can choose a rough path or a bright and easy path.

## THE MAZE

This is a wonderful story I was given many years ago, and it should give you great insight and may even change your life.

One morning, a young man came to the Master saying, "Master, I wish to understand my path on earth better. I wish to know why I continue to carry my past and re-live it. Why is it that I cannot get past my past?"

The Master smiled at the young man, who seemed to be earnest.

"Go forward into the Maze in the garden. But carry this backpack as you walk the maze. It will help you stay focused and balanced. Be careful, as it is quite heavy, though," the Master said.

The young man took the backpack from the Master, who handed it over quite easily. But when the young man had it firmly in his grasp, he was astonished at how heavy it really was! Placing the shoulder straps over his arms and bent over from the sheer weight of the pack, he strode the Maze.

He was surprised to see it was not a garden maze but was built of nearly translucent silk panels. The young man paused before entering the maze and then walked into it. Immediately, he found himself facing a solid wall of silk. However, he could see just enough through the silk to see other areas of the maze to make out others there simultaneously. He could "see" them and hear them, but they were not part of his path.

The weight upon his shoulders reminded him of why he was there, so he put the thoughts of the others out of his head. Walking forward, he found himself hopelessly trapped. It seemed that no matter which direction he walked, there was no way to proceed forward. Baffled, the young man sat down and pondered his situation.

The Master told me to walk the maze, but walking seemed impossible. Yet, there are others here who are obviously ahead of me. They must have figured out a way to get through this section. How did they do that? Are they smarter than I am? Did they cheat? Did they crawl under the silk, as that would be really a simple matter, and who would ever know? The young man weighed his options and then rose, deciding not to sneak under the silk. As he stood and turned, an opening appeared before him as though by magic, and he moved forward.

Soon, he faced another series of solid silk panels and could see no opening or direction to walk other than the one he had come from.

Again, he sat down and thought of his situation. He had gotten through the first test, he felt, by reflecting upon his options and then choosing to take the one that was for his highest good. Stating again his affirmation that he would desire to walk the maze only with positive intent, he stood, ready to face his opening.

But none was there. He still faced a blank series of panels. The young man was baffled. He had felt that surely, he would be rewarded as before for his desire to proceed only within his highest good.

The weight of his backpack cut into his shoulders, bringing him sharply back to reality. What was it that weighed so much? What had the Master placed in it to weigh it down? Rocks? Bricks? It did not feel hard and unforgiving like those items. It felt soft yet heavy. What could possibly be soft and yielding yet heavy enough to weigh him down like this? Pulling the backpack off his shoulders, he opened it and peeked inside. The Master did not tell him not to look, he reasoned. It was EMPTY! Yet it had weight! 'How could this be?' he wondered. Picking it back up, he again felt how heavy it was, yet it was empty! Again, he glanced inside and, this time, felt with his hands. Empty! But the weight!!! Placing it upon his shoulders, he stood. He asked himself what it was that he had just learned from this experience.

He heard a voice clearly say, *look inside of you, young man, for the weight lies there*. As he walked, he looked at his life and his path. He thought of his childhood and the friends and enemies who had caused him harm. He thought of how stuck he had been by their feelings for him and their attitudes towards him. He remembered how angry he was with one particular boy who had taunted him unmercifully. To this day, he still hates that young man. The backpack became even heavier as the student re-created and re-lived the experience within his mind and heart. "Ah. I understand now. I carry the weight of that which burdens me. I am the weight! I, therefore, have it within me to unburden myself as well", he said to himself.

The student was joyous with this insight and then saw and walked through a series of silk panels. He thought of how he could unburden the weight of those he still despised and resented for their treatment of him. He knew they were not there with him in the maze, so he could not expect them to say, "I am sorry," and thus lessen the weight and allow him to go forward easily.

"I forgive you, wherever you are," he found himself saying to his own amazement.

Fairy Tales, Dreams and Reality...

The weight of the pack lessened immediately, and he was able to walk without bending forward at the waist. 'Ah ha!' the young one exclaimed. Through my intent to forgive, I unburden myself of this weight that hinders my journey.

But how can this be? For they were the ones who wronged me, and yet my forgiving them un-weighs me. The young one's head swam with the implications as he did; another series of openings appeared before him in silk panels. His pack was considerably lighter but still weighed enough for his mind to stay focused on it.

"Oh, Great Spirit, I ask you to help me see what you are showing me here. How do I make my way through this maze? How do I release myself of the full weight that I carry with me?"

At that moment, a beam of sunlight hit him squarely in the face, warming him.

He suddenly realized his pack had lightened again with the sun's warmth! 'What does this mean, God? Why do you lighten my pack with sunlight? What are you showing me? Then, he found himself remembering a "woman" he had kissed when he was thirteen. It was his first kiss of adulthood, and he remembered her clearly. His heart raced with the remembrance of her taste upon his lips and his love for her. His pack lightened considerably this time.

"Thank you, God, for your considerable wisdom in this. I see now how I am to unburden myself completely. It is through my loving and forgiving those who have been in my way and have wronged me previously. It is not their wronging of me that has hindered me. It is my holding on to that wronging that has stopped me. I could not go forward in the maze by seeing myself as one who has been wronged. And by seeing myself as one without love, I could not lessen the weight of the pack. As I forgive and bring love within me, I make my journey easier."

The young man felt his heart swell as he felt these insights. He felt his heart race with joy as it knew its lesson to him was being heard.

The pack weighed nothing now, and the young man took it off and held it lightly. Standing before a solid silk wall now, he could see neither an opening nor his way to where he had just come from. He was surrounded by solid silk!

However, instead of panicking, he sat and breathed in this mantra; "I Am the light and the Way. I carry within me all manner of healing and knowing. Through this healing and knowing, I make my way through

Fairy Tales, Dreams and Reality...

this earthly maze. I am able to carry forth on the journey through this maze, and I am able to release my entrapment. I alone can solve this riddle, and I ask now to have it done. I breathe in full acceptance of my path and its possibilities, God. I recognized that I was the impediment, not anyone or anything else. I am LIGHT, and I am LOVE. Thus, being so FREES me and allows me to soar above the physical realm. In this re-discovery of myself, who is my True Self, God. Thank you for helping me to see this. I so love you."

At this, the young man felt his feet rise slightly above the earth! He floated above the silk panels and could clearly see the others stuck within the maze. Their darkness was being carried around in their own packs, holding them stuck. His head swam with the implications of what was happening to him at that moment. But he focused not on that but on the fact that he was flying! He was soaring! He was above the earth in his lightness! He was outside of the Maze!

Spying the ground around the maze, he thought of being there and staying outside of the maze. And at once, he was. By thinking about it and seeing it, it became. The Master was at his side as he touched down.

"Master, thank you for placing my weight so severely upon my shoulders as you did. Were it not so heavy, I would have gladly carried it longer and longer, for it would have not hindered me all that much. But as it weighed me down so greatly, I had to get rid of the weight first before I could do anything else."

"How did you free yourself of your weight, my son?" the Master asked. His face was alight with joy and love as he did so.

"I found myself forgiving those who had wronged me, Master. It was my pain in response to their actions that made me hold on to the pain inside of myself. When I let it go, Master, I watched as it soared away from me and felt myself growing lighter." The student's face shone with love as he spoke.

"AH," said the Master. "And what about the maze itself? That is impossible to walk through. There is no way out".

"Oh, Master. The most beautiful thing happened. I began to fly after losing weight. I saw myself as light and love as I found it within me to forgive and forget those who had harmed and wronged me. It was my darkness that had caused my weight, and my lightness freed me to fly. By BEING light and love, I floated Master and found myself outside the maze. I was freed from its confines above its entrapments. Master, I see now that my own weight holds me down, it keeps me trapped in my past. I alone am responsible for the manner in which I walk this maze. By releasing those entrapping thoughts, those weighing down feelings, and allowing myself to feel love and light, I soared above it all".

"Did I do wrong by getting out of the maze this way, Master?" The young man was earnest as he awaited the Master's answer.

"What do you feel, young one?" the Master answered with a smile, "Do you feel freed from the Maze?"

With that, the Master strode away before hearing the young one's reply. He knew that whatever the young one answered would give him further insight into his journey. And this is as it should be.

*Original Author Unknown*

Many other stories are similar to this one; another is "The Man in the maze," which is shared by many native tribes.

I believe we alone carry our burdens, and only we can free them.
*Karma is a reaction to our actions. Depending on how I (emotionally, spiritually, physically, or mentally) accept a situation, I will react to it repeatedly.

*Karma: In Buddhist teaching, the law of karma says only this: `For every event that occurs, there will follow another event whose existence was caused by the first, and this second event will be pleasant or unpleasant according to its cause was skillful or unskillful.

Fairy Tales, Dreams and Reality...

**"How are you going to change your path?"**

*One way is by dreaming... and letting our minds wander. The other is to watch what you ask for.*

Fairy Tales, Dreams and Reality...

# DREAMS:
## Wishes & Desires

*You need a starting point to accomplish change,*
*and dreaming of a new path is a great beginning!*

*"Dream Big!"*

Fairy Tales, Dreams and Reality...

# Dreams, Wishes & Desires

Literal meaning: dreaming usually happens during the REM sleep or alpha state and is a subconscious experience with images, sounds, ideas, and emotions. Twelve percent of people dream only in black and white.

Lucid dreaming is when the dreamer realizes that they are dreaming and can sometimes change their dream environment and control some aspects of the dream. When someone says they dream of a better life, job, partner, etc., they usually mean thinking of a better experience than they have now.

Many books and speakers discuss dreams or miracles coming true, like in *The Secret, Law of Attraction, or What the Bleep Do We Know*. This subject has been talked about since Jesus in the Bible, and I assume way before that. In all versions, positive thinking is used to create your destiny, which is the key.

It is true; negativity can only cloud your decisions or create indecision. No matter what is going on in your life, you must have some big dreams. No matter how crazy or unbelievable they may seem, you need to have a few big ones and some realistic ones.

When you were a kid, you may have been lying on your back on the soft green grass in a park you played in or maybe on a beach one warm summer day, and you were daydreaming about your future. Think, feel, or visualize what you would be when you grow up, who you would marry, what your children would look like, or what you would get for Christmas.

When life is simple, and we have time on our hands…we have time to dream. Many of us in today's world work full time, have kids at home, and many other responsibilities, leaving us no extra time to breathe, let alone dream.

When life takes a bump, it might be because you did not give yourself time, so the universe gave the time to you, so you would have to make time; there is no choice. An example would be an accident, and you are bedridden for a few weeks or months.

## Achieving your Dreams

To achieve your dreams…it will all depend on how badly you want, desire, or wish for them and what you will do to get it...The law of attraction is easy; think about it, and it will be…the reality is…the pain you are feeling is usually the only reason that you will change.

*Dreams are today's answers to tomorrow's questions.*
*Edgar Cayce*

Here are some ways for you to make time and have the chance to dream.

Experiences like.
    Exercise
    Holidays
    Hobbies
    Hypnosis
    Meditation

These all let us go into an alpha state by doing them and will give us time for dreaming. You can also take classes or buy tapes that can guide you into a dream state so that your mind can relax, and your worries can disappear for a few moments to remember how to dream.

Following are more experiences to try and improve or change your path...

#### #1) Meditation Exercise:

You can recite a wonderful meditation into a tape recorder or have someone read to you. A great experience is listening while you are in the bathtub or before you sleep.

Say the following meditation using a slow, relaxing voice (and every time '...' appears, wait a few moments before saying the following line):

    Make yourself comfortable...

For the next few breaths, notice your breathing and how you take that breath...

Count in your head how long it takes to take a breath, in and out...

Now count how long you can hold between the in... and out... breath...

As you continue to breathe, let out any negative thoughts or feelings ...

    Notice your toes...

    You may even wiggle them...

    Great...

Take a deep breath all the way down to the tip of your toes and let go of any pain or negative energy being held in your toes...

Now focus on your ankles…

Again, let go of any pain or negative energy being held there…

Release and relax…

Focus now on your calves and knees…

And thighs…

Let go of any negative energy being held there also…

Let go…

Relax and release…

Moving up to your hips…

Breathe it all out…

Your torso…

Including all the organs inside …

And every vertebra in your spinal column…

Release and let go…

Notice your shoulders…

Arms…

Hands and fingers…

Breathe all the way to the tips and release…

Moving up to your neck…

Take a deep breath and release any tension there also…

Notice your head…

Take a breath, relax, and release any negative energy in your…

Face…cheeks, lips…

Eyes, ears, and nose…

Great…

Now that you have relaxed your physical body…

Let's relax your mental body…

In a moment, you will start to count down in your mind from 100…

With each number you will relax twice as much as you were before…

Go ahead…100…

Deep breath…

99…

98…

97…

Okay…now, at this stage of your relaxation, just let all the remaining numbers disappear…

Great…

Now, imagine you have a box that has a lockable lid…
If you have any negative thoughts…
Feelings…
Words…
Tastes…
Images…
Or smells…
Let them all go into the box…

…

…

Now that the negative energy is in the box…
Close the lid…
And place the lock into the latch…
Now you have a choice…
You can store the box for safe keeping…
Or the box will just vanish forever…
Your choice…
Great…

In a moment, you will teleport yourself into a relaxing hammock…
Or lounge…
Knowing the weather is just perfect…
You love the temperature…
Relaxing and just letting yourself daydream…
Your dreams are very enjoyable…

…

You start to notice your toes…
And slightly wiggle them as you come back to the moment and real-world…
You stretch as you open your eyes…
Feeling rejuvenated and wonderful…
If you want more insight into why you do not have what you desire…you can adjust the meditation to:
The weather outside is just perfect…
You love the temperature…
Relaxing and just dreaming…

You ask yourself, what do I need to know, feel, see or hear…

To understand what is blocking my dreams, wishes or desires? …

From coming true...

*All our dreams can come true if we have the courage to pursue them. Walt Disney*

The castle in Princeton

## Achieving your Dreams

### #2) How to make your dreams/ wishes/ desires come true.

I was meditating one day, and my intent or question was, 'How do we manifest or create our desires, wishes, or dreams into reality? Here is what I came up with, and is a section from one of my courses I teach:

### Scenario #1

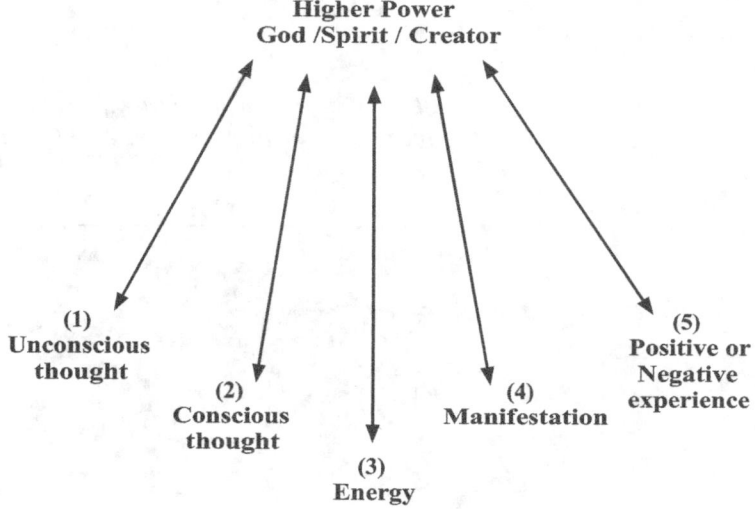

**Unconscious thought:** which is quick and not really taken as anything important, a thought pops in and then out of your mind in a split second. You never think of it again.

> For example, you are at work, and while working, you have a brief thought of being in Mexico, not giving it another thought.

> • Spirit hears this information but pays no attention; millions of unconscious thoughts are heard each second (The arrows show the direction of information traveling both ways).

**Conscious thought:** This is something that is repeatedly thought about and in more detail.

*A few weeks later, a friend said he was going to Mexico and asked if you could go along. You go home and think about it.*

- Again, Spirit hears this conscious thought and starts to pay attention to you.

Energy is when you put more than thought into an idea. You may tell someone about it, write it down, and start the process with tangible effort.

*You decide to get the information from a travel agent and look it over. The next day, you talk it over again with your friends and choose to put a deposit on the trip. And now you start to tell your co-workers and friends that you are going to Mexico.*

- Again, Spirit can see, hear, feel, and know you are serious.

4) Manifestation: Successful manifestation is when you achieve your original outcome.

*You actually land in Mexico for your trip.*

- Spirit will provide what we ask for. Literally, what we ask for and believe we deserve. So be careful what you ask for! Or ask it to be for your higher good and best interest.

5) Positive or negative: This is the most important part of the process, determining if the manifestation was a positive or negative experience.

*Many people have a one-time wish (desire or dream); an example would be to go and have a week or two in Mexico, and once that is accomplished, they never need to think about the wish again. Where others have a wish and would like that wish to be forever (to live in Mexico forever). Then there are others who wish they lived there, and then after a few months of being there, the fantasy is gone, and the reality is worse than where they came from in the first place.*

In this step of the process, the cycle will be determined if the manifestation starts all over again by the outcome of your experience. Was it a good or bad experience? Good thoughts keep continuing to manifest, and bad thoughts sabotage it.

- Remember, Spirit helps you achieve whatever you ask, good or bad.

- **If you have any emotional issues or negative thoughts about the experience, these will sabotage the process to work again or keep the wish.**

- **Suppose your thought patterns are always genuine and positive on the manifested wish. In that case, you will always** keep the manifestation until you decide to manifest something else that you would like to replace it with.

• If you are not receiving what you want, go get help and clear the issues that are standing in your way of getting what you want.

**Scenario #2**

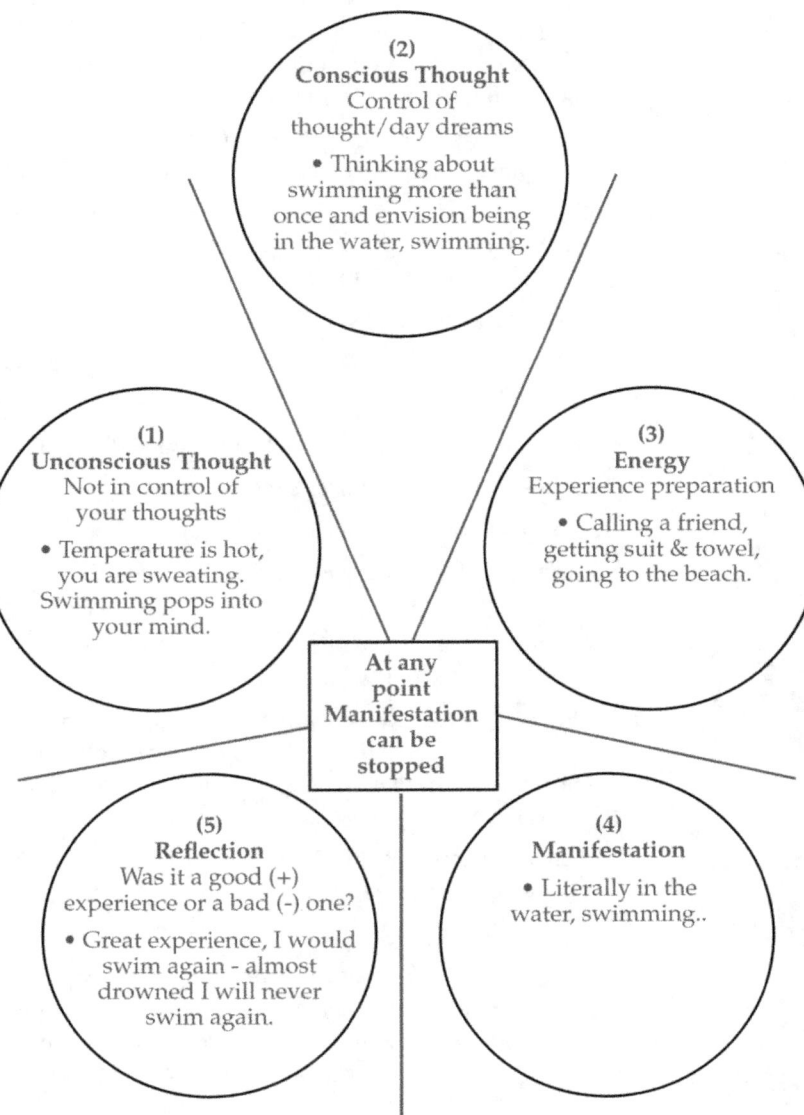

**(2)**
**Conscious Thought**
Control of
thought/day dreams

• Thinking about
swimming more than
once and envision being
in the water, swimming.

**(1)**
**Unconscious Thought**
Not in control of
your thoughts

• Temperature is hot,
you are sweating.
Swimming pops into
your mind.

**(3)**
**Energy**
Experience preparation

• Calling a friend,
getting suit & towel,
going to the beach.

**At any
point
Manifestation
can be
stopped**

**(5)**
**Reflection**
Was it a good (+)
experience or a bad (-) one?

• Great experience, I would
swim again - almost
drowned I will never
swim again.

**(4)**
**Manifestation**

• Literally in the
water, swimming..

This diagram shows you the same five step cycle with a different scenario.

1. Imagine you are working outside, and it is very hot. You have a brief moment of thought of swimming. It passes quickly, and you do not continue to think about swimming.

2. A couple of hours later, it is really hot out, and you are sweating. This time you think about swimming with your friend.

3. Ten minutes later you call her and ask if she wants to go swimming with you and she agrees. You finish work, go home to collect your swimsuit and towel, pick up your friend, and head off to the beach.

4. You are in the water swimming.

5. You finish swimming, drop off your friend, and head home.

During any scenario, you could have stopped the process at any stage:

1. A co-worker hurts himself, and you have to take him to the hospital.

2. It starts to rain, and you are not hot any longer.

3. Your friend says that another friend has invited you to a party; it sounds more fun, so you choose to attend the party instead.

4. Your car breaks down, or maybe the road is blocked, so you do not get to the beach to swim.

5. Your friend has never swum before, and you both almost drowned. She had a bad experience and vowed never to swim again due to fear; you have swum hundreds of times and just put it down to bad luck and continue to swim in the future.

There are many ways to create your dreams. But first, you need to know what your dreams are.

*No one should negotiate their dreams.*
*Dreams must be free to fly high. No government, no*
*legislature, has a right to limit your dreams.*
*You should never agree to surrender your dreams.*

**Jesse Jackson**

Fairy Tales, Dreams and Reality...

## Achieving your Dreams

### #3) Exercise: 100 goals

*(or as you may know it since the movie Bucket List)* Write out one hundred different things/goals to accomplish before death, not just ten or fifty... one hundred. It does not matter if you believe you can or cannot accomplish them, just write them down.

I have been told, many times, that if you put pen in hand and write your thoughts on paper, your brain chemistry changes and starts to create your reality.

*Have you ever owned or driven a vehicle, and all you see is that vehicle make, model, and/or color around town, and then you buy a different vehicle, and now all you see is the new one all over town and have forgotten about the other one you had just owned? Your brain is amazing. It is like the law of attraction: what you think you will attract.*

Ideas that you can use to write about:
- all the places you want to visit...each one counts
- what kind of house you want
- furniture
- toys
- accomplishments
- hobbies you would like to do
- any volunteer work
- public speaking arrangements
- bungee jumping
- jumping out of an airplane

Anything you can think of, write it down...it could take a couple of weeks...time is not the issue, and later, if you want to, you can add to it as your complete items.

After you have completed writing down 100 things...the odds are that you will accomplish more than eighty percent. Most of my students and clients notice a change almost instantly. You can do this with any individual goal:
- House renovations: write down everything to be redone, room by room.
- Vehicle, Job: Type, pay, position
- Trip, write out fine details

*Ensure you have set up your rules or guidelines with God/ creator/spirit before writing your goals.*

An example of some rules: when I achieve my goals or whatever I do,

- **I cannot go bankrupt**
- **Cause a divorce**
- **Interfere with my family life in any negative way that will cause harm to the manifestations I already have in place that take priority.**

Once you have written out your dreams, wishes, and desires, it is time to find out what is stopping you. In the following pages are ideas for you to use to clear the negative and bring forth your dreams!

**#4) To attract your Perfect mate: Write out 100 things you want in a perfect mate. Details!!!**

Ideas: Anything that is important to you
- Their looks
    - ~ Hair color
    - ~ Eye color
    - ~ Height
    - ~ Weight
    - ~ Clothes
- Want children or not
    - ~ If so, how many
- Hobbies
    - ~ Art
    - ~ Reading
    - ~ Games
    - ~ Sports
    - ~ TV/movies
- Politics
- Jobs
    - ~ Travel or at home
    - ~ Income
    - ~ Care if you work or not
- Family (in-laws /outlaw) like or does not matter
- Addictions
    - ~ Cigarette smoker
    - ~ Drugs
    - ~ Alcohol
    - ~ Food
    - ~ Gambling

- Sex
- Trips or Holidays
- How they drive
- Lying / truth, honesty
- On-time
- Amount of time spent together
- Friends
- Personal belongings
- How they treat you

- Vehicle they drive
- Where to live
    - ~ Location
        - ~ House / Apartment
- Money
    - ~ Spending
    - ~ Saving
    - ~ Retirement

Note:   The rule is that after dating your partner for at least three months, if he/she does not match at least 80% of those criteria, find someone else!

Life is too short to be with someone you do not have much in common. Guilt from religion or society (family/friends) has made it a bit difficult to get out of a marriage / intimate relationship once you find out that he/she is not the right person for you. So it is much easier to do your homework!

**Write out your 100 requirements**…because you have to live with your decisions or choices, and it takes a bit of work to heal from the wrong path choice.

**#5) Here is an exercise to find out what might be stopping you from achieving your dreams or goals: Have a goal in mind that you would like to become a reality, and write down your answer to the following questions.**

What will you get from achieving your goal?

_____

_____

What stops you from achieving your dream today?

_____

_____

If you achieved your dream, what or who would it negatively affect?
Examples: Family, material items, job, etc.

_____

_____

How will your present situation, behaviors, and beliefs affect your 100
goals (values)? *Example: Goal to travel but have a six-month-old
child.*

_____

_____

What do you feel (what emotion) when you don't achieve your goal?

_____

_____

Once you have answered the questions above, you may notice a pattern
or excuse for not achieving your goal(s) and can use that to move
forward. It is hard to move forward if you do not know what is causing
your problems. A person with an addiction can only heal once they
admit they are one.

I have flipped a coin in the past (heads 'yes,' tails 'no') to make a
decision. It was not the heads or tails I would listen to; it was how I
felt with the answer. Was I happy, sad, or relieved? How I feel is
usually how I make my decision... was I happy when it was a 'no?'
Then, of course, do not do it. But if you feel differently than the
answer, if it says 'no' and you are very upset at the answer, listen to
your feelings!

**Pleasure and Pain...**

**How bad does it have to get before you change?**

Many magazines, web sites and trade shows advertise practitioners and courses or seminars. Meditation, hypnosis, and self-esteem or self-improvement courses and programs can all get you back on track. Look up practitioners in your telephone book: alternative practitioners under health and healing, individual headings, hypnosis, or counselor. Your local health food store new age store should be able to guide you to the right person or program. Books are a great source for change.

I enjoy taking new courses and having another perspective on how to do something or think about something. Sometimes, I need a whammy course, a real wake-up course that challenges me to get motivated and/or move my garbage, which is blocking me from doing and believing what is needed!

*So many of our dreams at first seem impossible, then they seem improbable, and when we summon the will, they soon become inevitable.*

*Christopher Reeve*

# More Ways to Improve Your

# Health, Wealth & Happiness

# HEALTH

*Without health, life is not life;*
*it is only a state of languor and suffering - an image of death.*

**Buddha**

**Health**

Everyone says, "Eat right and exercise." Of course, we all know we are what we eat.

I could go on forever on what makes us healthy. There are millions of books written on the subject. But do we follow or listen… In Dr. Willard's herb course, there was a cartoon drawing of a lady who looked like a hippy from the Woodstock days sitting on a park bench, eating a healthy salad. Beside her was a businessman dressed in his suit and tie with a briefcase on the ground beside his feet, eating a quick drive-through juicy beef hamburger. She looked at him eating his meal with disgust, and he seemed oblivious to anyone beside him on the park bench. He had his face held up to the warm sun, enjoying the well-deserved lunch break, and looked like nothing in the world was more beautiful than this moment.

From this picture, I understood to be careful about what you think while eating.

It is proven that the tears from your eyes caused by crying can change pH due to your emotions, and if you are eating healthy but thinking bad thoughts, your pH can change to a more acidic pH and cause you to become ill even though you are eating healthy.

In chemistry, pH measures the acidity or basicity of a solution. The scale that is used for measuring the pH or hydrogen ion concentration … is from 0 to 14, with 7 being the neutral point. Pure water is considered neutral, with a pH close to 7.0 at 25 °C (77 °F). Solutions with a pH less than 7 are said to be acidic, and solutions with a pH greater than 7 are said to be basic or alkaline.

The healthy or optimal pH of the body's fluids, such as the blood urine, is 7.4, slightly alkaline. Outside of this range … the body activity is no longer optimal, and the metabolism is out of balance. A more acidic body attracts pathogens (viral, bacterial, fungal, or parasitic). When you are more acidic, you are telling the universe that you are dying, and the pathogen's job is to come and decompose. Pathogens are very good at their job.

With previous experience owning a café, I had the pleasure of serving people healthy, nourishing food...I will tell you right now that healthy foods did not sell. I had all kinds of salads and good-for-you foods, and they sat there and went bad. What I thought would be good to sell and what sells are two different things.

People are coming in for a break, usually a quick break from work, and have a very limited amount of time. They have been working hard, and what seems to attract people is the goodies, cookies, and muffins. Of course, caffeine is a big thing and sells well. Even the soups were the yummy kind, not the healthy kind. And if the weather, stock market, time change, or a holiday is that week, believe me, I am the first to know. Customers are very finicky with their eating when change happens.

Don't forget what controls the body...you may ask yourself:

• What is the most protected part of your body? *Most people answer that it is the organs inside their rib cage or spinal column. Really think about what is so protected... It is your brain! The thickness, solidness, and size of bones that protect it are amazing.*
• What is the last system to stop working when we die? Yes, it is the brain.
• What does the brain need to function?... Sugar

No wonder most crave sweets or foods that turn into sugar, like carbohydrates. We always think the brain will protect itself from other organs or systems. When it is not fed, it will control you until you feed it, or it will steal from other systems to get what it needs, and then your health will pay the price.

Don't you find it interesting that even though they say that we are eating so unhealthily and that we are the most obese society ever in history, though interestingly, we are living the longest in all history? One reason is that machines and technology have made our physical lives easier. Not as much stress on our bodies as in the past. Medicine and medical alternatives have improved by leaps and bounds. On average, each household is making more money in history than ever before. We own more toys and go on more holidays than at any other time in history. Even blue-collar workers are now regularly pampering themselves like famous stars.

### #6) Simple ways to help you.

a) Think as positively as possible, and do not judge others! You are what you think, and who wants to be negative because of someone else's habits?

b) Take time to smell the roses. Remember to enjoy life…as my mother would say, "What is the alternative"?

c) Breathing…deep breathing can help make you healthy…oxygen is needed in all body parts. Make sure you breathe deep, tummy breaths not just short little ones.

d) Of course, you still need to eat your veggies and a variety of foods for optimal nutrient intake. Eat what is correct for you and not just because your friend is on some new diet, so you are too.

e) Move that body, even slightly, for lymphatic and blood circulation.

f) Keep trying to learn something new…expand and change your neuron pathways, and you will keep that mind young.

# WEALTH

*There are people who have money and people who are rich.*
*Coco Chanel*

### Wealth

I guess I do not hold onto money. All you need to do is look at the economy in 2008 (the stock market crash) to see that we have a disaster without money circulating.

I was having a class discussion about beliefs about money in the business course that I teach.

To me, it is paper, and what is real is what it buys. I have big goals... I know that is my secret (I write down all my goals), and then I do silly things (well, others may think they are silly) like:

• Pulling up the old carpet in my home before I have the money to buy new floors.

• I send post-dated cheques to people and when they have all the money, I get what I want to buy.

• I have borrowed on high-interest loans.

• I wanted a castle...and achieved that dream, even if it didn't last long.

### #7) Wealth Exercise:

...Write out as many beliefs as you have about money. They can be good or bad, from birth to now. Example:

| I love money | There is never enough |
| Money buys me what I desire | We are poorer than my friends |
| **Good Beliefs** | **Bad Beliefs** |

_____    _____

_____    _____

_____    _____

_____    _____

_____    _____

_____    _____

_____    _____

_____    _____

_____    _____

_____    _____

_____    _____

_____    _____

_____    _____

_____    _____

Just remember that any negative issues that you have, like bankruptcy, divorce, personal pleasure, food, shelter, etc., are detrimental to your well-being and will determine (override) any dream, wish, want, or desire you may have.

> _If there is even one person that means something to you and they do not want the same thing for you, they might be able to cancel out your achievement, and then your wish, dream, or desire may not happen._

This works like the 'Hundred Monkey Theory' just in reverse. The hundred-monkey theory had to do with one monkey that decided to wash its food before eating it. As time passed, another monkey started to wash its food first, and then another, and so on. It was noted that as time passed on a totally different island, the monkeys there started to wash their food before eating it, too.

So again, the thoughts of others can cause a reversal on your dream; if you have a dream and you say it out loud and one person, especially if they are someone important to you, does not like a dream and then another person and another. You will most likely give up on your dream due to the hundred-monkey effect.

### #8) Wealth Exercise:

To discover your subconscious issues about money (we call this story mode) ...Lie down or sit comfortably. Really, all you need to do is relax, let your mind drift, and imagine what it will.

Go into meditation:

For the next few breaths, notice your breathing and how you take that breath...

Count in your head how long it takes to take a breath in and out...

Now count how long you can hold between the in... and out... breath...

As you breathe, let out any negative thoughts or feelings ...

Notice your toes...

You may even wiggle them...

Great...

Take a deep breath all the way down to the tip of your toes and let go of any pain or negative energy being held in your toes...

Now focus on your ankles...

Again, let go of any pain or negative energy being held there...

Release and relax...

Focus on your calves, knees...

And thighs...

Let go of any negative energy being held there also...

Let go...

Relax and release...

Moving up to your hips...

Breathe it all out...

Your torso...

Including all your organs...

And every vertebra in your spinal column...

Release and let go...

Notice your shoulders...

Arms...

Hands and fingers...

Breathe all the way to the tips and release...

Moving up to your neck...

Take a deep breath and release any tension there also…
 Notice your head…
Take a breath, relax, and release any negative energy in your…
Cheeks, lips…
Eyes, ears, and nose…
Great…
I know my mind will put me right into story mode (like a movie
script) and give me a wonderful story so that I can learn
what my financial blocks are caused from…
Show me who I was in the story?...
What did I do for a living?...
How did I earn my money?....
Who controlled the money?....
What happened to the money?....
What do I need to know to be able to change my money habits?...

You can do this exercise many times and have different stories. The
information you get will give you the underlying subconscious
meaning of your path, financially or any other.

This knowledge will help you determine how to release the negative
memories in your mind's story, if any. If you noticed a distinct smell
from memory (maybe you're a teacher's perfume and you hated that
teacher), you would want to activate (remember) the scent and release
the emotional thoughts simultaneously as the smell.

When you are asking questions in your mind to think of more details,
just ask yourself what you are:
 Seeing? Hearing? Feeling? Smelling? Tasting?

*I've failed over and over and over again in my life, and
that is why I succeeded.*

*Michael Jordan*

# HAPPINESS

*Most folks are about as happy as they make
up their minds to be. Abraham
Lincoln*

## Happiness

People's perceptions on this topic are very controversial.

What is happiness?
  A state of mind or feeling such as contentment, satisfaction, pleasure,
  or joy

**Happiness from my perspective:** This is how I see myself and my
immediate family, and I am sure there are many other things that they
would write down or even maybe erase.

What makes me happy?
  Creating, challenges, improving my Emotional, Mental, Spiritual,
  Physical growth, my family, beautiful things, dreaming, writing,
  teaching, traveling, reading, art, food, TV, animals, innocence of
  children, laughter, gifts, surprises, seeing a loved one, the movies,
  comedy, dancing, sex, working, swimming, tennis, skiing, cards,
  games, stories, computer, trees, plants, stars, planets, building,
  selling, making, hobbies, pretty things, sounds of music.

What makes my husband happy?
  Money, work, sex, food, getting compliments, playing baseball,
  tennis, volleyball, skiing, boating, building nice things, TV,
  relaxing, the internet.

What makes my son happy?
  Games, his friends, food, family outings, his girlfriend, challenging
  education, science, sports, boating, computer, TV.

What makes my daughter happy?
  My daughter says it is sunshine!

Make-up, nails, work, money, her dog and cat, her friends, her family, graduating with her friends, boating, clothes, and talking on the internet.

What makes my mom happy?
Family getting along, work, travel, the card game bridge, family dinners, making things, taking off to Arizona, boating in the sun.

What do I see that makes some of my other family members happy?
Helping the poor, friends, cooking, gardening, dancing, reading, writing, drinking and drugs.

#9) Write out what makes you happy.

_____

**You are whatever you believe you are and whatever you will put up with.**
...pleasure and pain.

**Here are some more ideas that you can use to create happiness in your life:**

## Muscle Testing
Many holistic practitioners use muscle testing. Many people use it for their own benefit of answering a 'yes' or 'no' question.

You will need to program your body to be able to move to an answer to a 'yes' or 'no' question. Your brain is like a computer and needs to be programmed in order to give you an honest answer.

### #10) Muscle Testing Exercise:
• Stand upright.
• Literally move your body forward (moving from the ankles, keeping a straight body, like a two x four piece of wood), saying, "Forward is a 'yes.'"
• Literally move your body backward, saying, "Backwards is a 'no' without falling."
• Do both yes and no movements three times each. This programs your subconscious brain to be able to move your body for the correct answer.
• You may have to soften or let go of your knees a bit (it will control the movement if the knees are locked in too tightly). • Now try saying, "My name is ___?_____." (Put in your real first name).

Your answer with your real name should have made your body go forward without you trying to.

• Now say a wrong name, "My name is ___?_____." When using a false name, your body should have moved backward.

• If your body moves from side to side, it usually means you should ask a better or more detailed question.

• The body not moving means it does not know the answer.    Practice makes perfect. Make sure you know your body moves correctly, test it many times over a few days, and if it always answers correctly, you have programmed it enough to trust it on more difficult answers.

You can use this technique for as many personal questions as you like.

Whenever you have a decision to make, it is a great way to get the answer.

I have used it:

• To decide if my child should go somewhere or do something. I would have her write out her question (that way, she can never say something else), and I test it. Even if I think it is not the answer I would have given, I trust the muscle testing to be accurate. You can always ask more detailed questions.

• To pick between two or more items

• To even ask if I should buy something

• In healing, I have asked which system of the body is creating the issue or if it is chemical, emotional, etc.

• Anything at all


**Things that make us laugh.**

   Laughter is a great modality in healing.

Remember, it is proven that the pH level (pH is the acid / alkaline level in the body) of a teardrop from your eye will change with your moods, with more acid when you are sad and more alkaline when you are happy.

   *Did you hear of the guy whose mother wanted to commit suicide? She was only joking.*

Funny? Not usually, especially when you can imagine it happening in real life and can relate it to something real. Some thoughts bring us down. Notice how fast your energy level changes.

   *Did you hear of the guy whose mother forgot she had hair rollers in her hair and went out shopping?*


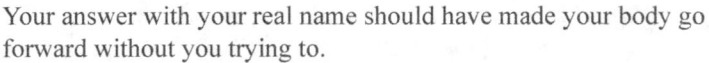
Fairy Tales, Dreams and Reality...

See how fast our images can change and bring more happiness.

*Did you hear of the guy whose mother was a man?*

I can keep you thinking whatever I want…but only if you keep reading. People only read what they like and watch only what they like…

Laughter is in the emotions of the beholder. One person can find something hysterically funny, whereas another may only smile, and another get annoyed.

Laughter creates endorphins in the body that work as natural painkillers, producing a general sense of well-being. Laughter also helps to lower blood pressure, reduces stress, increases muscle flexion, and boosts immune function.

Incorporate laughter into your day by reading comics, watching TV, going out with friends, or going to a comedy show. Some courses teach laughter, and you have to fake it until you make it.

*Ha, Ha, Ha…*

**I am thankful for laughter, except when**
**milk comes out of my nose.**

**Woody Allen**

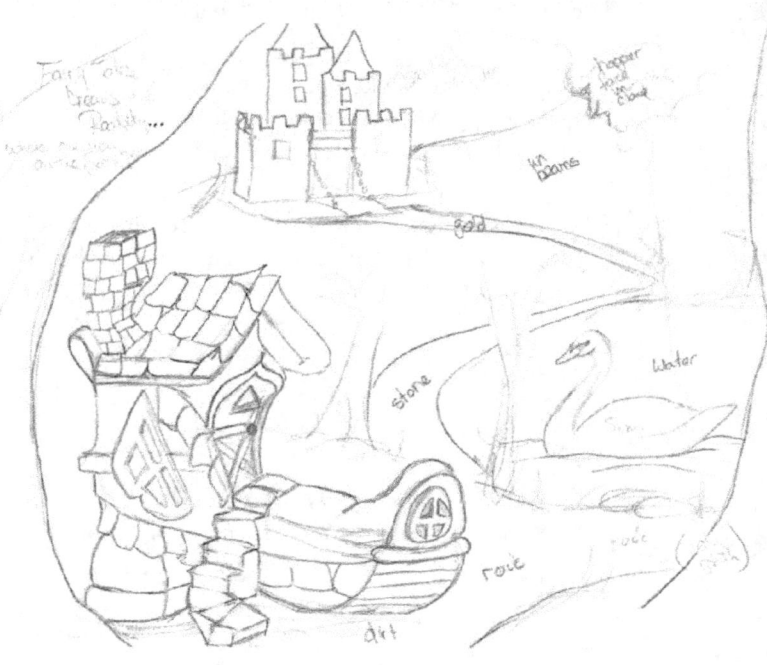

*My original concept/drawing that I gave Jennifer for the reality of this book cover to be created.*

Fairy Tales, Dreams and Reality...

# REALITY

*The shadow is what we think of it; the tree is the real thing.*
*Abraham Lincoln*

# Reality. . . Truth or Fact

How often do you walk down the street and touch the car, tree, or dog you just passed to find out if it is real? I doubt you do…you just believe it is real. You saw it and might have even heard it, so you believe it is real!

Most of us know the difference between a fairy tale, dream, or reality.

- A fairy tale is a made-up, far-fetched, enchanted story.
- A dream is a subconscious experience, usually in your sleep (but can also be a daydream), with all the sensations of being real.
- Reality is anything you can prove to be true or fact.

*A teacher told me about an incident that happened to his student. The guy was driving along a winding mountain highway. The side of the road he was driving on had a very sharp edge and dropped a couple hundred feet. The student was just coming into a left curve in the road when an oncoming vehicle seemed to be out of control and coming straight for him. As the student took a deep breath (of fear for his life or to change his destiny), the oncoming vehicle crossed his lane in front of him, and before the vehicle went over the edge, it vanished into thin air.*

*Shaken from the experience, he wanted to pull over. As it was unsafe to stop, the student continued to drive a little further ahead and pulled over as soon as possible. He didn't even have a chance to get out of his vehicle and run back to really see what happened when a knock on his driver's side window came and a man, who had been following in the car behind him, was frantically saying, 'Oh my God, did you see that... it just vanished!*

Just because YOU do not believe it doesn't mean it is not truth or fact!

**Fact**: a thing known to be true. Fact: the sun rises in the East

This fact is provable anywhere in the world by people belonging to any group or nationality, regardless of which language they speak or which part of the hemisphere they come from.

Things as they actually exist: emotionally, spiritually, mentally, and physically. Something you can feel, see, touch, and hear or prove to be fact by all.

**Truth** is when two or more people agree upon an event or experience.

An example would be how many different versions of the bible there are and how many different religions believe theirs to be the true meaning.

Many of us *never* question authority and believe whatever we are taught or told.

Yet most of us grow up believing...lies. Yes, I wrote lies.

Did you grow up believing in the Tooth Fairy, Santa Claus, Easter Bunny, or any other character? Do you remember how disappointed you were when you found out the truth? If you have grown up in a Christian religion, there again, you may not have all the facts. Did you know that a man has the same number of ribs as a woman?

If it is not the truth or a fact, then it is considered a lie, and the only difference between a joke and a lie is that you smile or laugh after you tell a joke.

*What influences our decisions or path choices in life... truth, facts, or lies?*

When we are born, a path is created for us, one that our parents have, and it is not until later in life that we have the choice to stay on the same path or to choose another one.

As kids, most of us were allowed to imagine almost anything and had so much fun pretending to be those things. Like many other young children, I loved to fantasize, play dress up and act out, or dream about what I saw on TV, read in a book, or overhear my parents and family talk about what they called 'adult talk'.

Yesterday and today: Barbie dolls, GI Joes, and many other toys are used for just that reason: to pretend or imagine that you are something you are not or to build something you do not have. Children's toys seem to be made for children to feel all grown up to help expand their imaginations.

Fairy Tales, Dreams and Reality...

I had many dolls to pretend I was a mom and Lego building blocks to build my house or anything else I could think of. I had all kinds of cool things like Lite-Bright, the game operation, and magic tricks. I would gather with my friends and cousins to playhouse, doctor, school, or church. We would pretend for hours we were the wife, husband, baby, teacher, student, doctor, patient, priest, or parishioner. With my guy friends, I would even play Cops and Robbers or Cowboys and Indians.

I remember spending hours looking at old Sears and Bay catalogs for the perfect people, furniture, wardrobe, and even children and then cutting them out so I could play… imagining I was all grown up and had all these beautiful things.

As we age, though, it is looked down upon us if we still fantasize about such things… unless you become an actor, then you are in character. At the age of twelve, I remember my mom telling me that I was now too old to play with Barbie dolls and I should give all my toys to my younger cousins. I remember being heartbroken that I had to give up my favorite playthings and grow up. After giving up my childhood toys, I went to TV, read books, and went out with my friends to entertain myself. Later, I remember pretending to smoke, drink alcohol, and even make out…oops…that was not pretending.

As adults, we are expected to grow up and have it all together: family, house, good job, and no problems…

As we get older, fantasizing and imagination are considered a waste of time. Many people find it too scary to tell his/her dreams or fantasies out loud and take a chance to be judged by family, friends, and acquaintances as crazy and unrealistic thoughts. Unfortunately, I have found that more people will give you their opinion of what they think about your intentions and may tell you that you need a total reality check and how stupid your idea is. Unless asked what they think, they should just listen and keep their opinions to themselves.

I have found that people with a very powerful voice and attitude, determination, and/or history of success will receive positive interest from others for their ideas.

How you present yourself will depend upon your childhood path, how you grew up, and how you respond to other people's reactions or comments. Were you taught that you had to respect your Elders? How did you react to being bullied? Were you a self-leader and did not need the approval of others? How did you handle criticism?

In reality, most people listening to a story of someone's personal wishes, wants, and desires will respond first by scanning their own life experiences and reacting in a way that they can understand or that is real to them. To make it worse, your so-called friends may tell you one thing, but behind your back, tell other people how they really feel about what you told them.

I find it interesting how a child, young adult, or seventy-year-old may tell a person a similar dream, and each one will get a bit of a different reaction just because of their age. The child is dreaming, the teenager is young and immature, and the older person is senile. Or is it that the child is pretending to be something, and it is cute? The teenager is determining his/her own path, and the old person is still senile.

When my daughter turned nineteen, she was making plans for her future. She joined a Network marketing (multi-level marketing) business and had such energy and excitement over the possibilities it WOULD bring her. Unfortunately, it was not long until she found that too many people did not want to be like her and join the network business as she did.

She also bought a couple of magazines on house plans. These particular houses started at one million dollars. Beautiful dream homes, and her showing me made me smile. Why did I smile? I guess it is because when I was her age, I was told to be realistic and think about a real home to buy.

My grandfather used to tell me I had champagne taste on a beer budget. When we were together, my husband would not let me look beyond his belief of a price range for our first house. I could not bring myself to live in the home he wanted to buy. I knew that with the way he was brought up and was used to, we might live in that house forever. Therefore, we started in a mobile home because I knew he would not live in a mobile home for long, and slowly we made our way up to a very nice home with a pool in the backyard.

But when I went for a castle, it was past his and many of my family member's reality.

**So, what influences us to make our decisions in life? Our path choices?**

Good question…what does make us choose our path? Or maybe a better question is…why are we questioning our current path choice?

**Path definition:**
A walkway is made by continual use, the direction in which a person/ thing is moving, or a course of action.

We all grew up taking a different path. Every human, even identical twins, has their own path. I believe that even if I were cloned, my cloned self would never be like me. She would never know the same father, mother, or friends as I did. She would not have fallen on that apple juice can and been blinded in the left eye at the age of one and a half, been abused by her father, fallen in love with my husband, or given birth to my two children. No, in today's world, she would have grown up with video games that are played on TV or live on the internet with other people, DVDs, CDs, computers, iPods, cell phones, a Hummer H2, and her best friend would be Facebook on the internet. She would not have any of my scars or memories. Maybe she would grow up in another country, speak a different language, and have an accent. No, our paths would not be the same;

Fairy Tales, Dreams and Reality…

she might not even look like me. Maybe she would have a different hairstyle or wear blue-colored contact lenses. She may never have had children or gained the weight I did after I had mine; maybe she had plastic surgery… totally different paths.

> *I was told a story by a speaker at one of his seminars many years ago, and it still holds my attention… it goes something like this: Many years ago, he was on a guided tour in the jungle. He was the last one in the line on the overgrown path. And due to the warm weather, he wore shorts, a shirt, and sandals.*
>
> *As he followed the group through the jungle, a bug bit him on the foot. He kept following the others to their destination without thinking anything of it. It was hard to see much in front or behind due to the thick foliage, so no one noticed the distance that had started to develop between him and the rest of the group.*
>
> *He said that he remembered following the other Doctors, and then the next thing he remembered was waking up to a stranger's blurry face staring at him. When his group and the interpreter were finally brought to him, he found out that he had been bitten by a poisonous ant, had gone into anaphylactic shock, and had passed out.*
>
> *The speaker asked the stranger, who turned out to be a medicine man from a nearby tribe, how he had found him. The Medicine man answered that there was a ripple in the jungle and went to see what had caused it. The speaker asked what had caused the ripple, and the man said… 'It was you'."*

I find it very interesting that the medicine man noticed a problem in the jungle and went to see what was causing it. Interestingly, one person's path and choice can affect more than we realize.

My dreams can affect my family; what if I move away? They may not get to see or be with me as much. If I open a restaurant, I might be working more than I used to and can no longer be home at night. Quit my job and be a stay-at-home mom. I would not have the income they are used to anymore.

I believe our good and bad experiences influence us, and our reactions seem to control our next steps in creating our future.

**Pleasure and pain...**

**We live for pleasure and will do almost anything to get out of pain...**

We all have a choice of which path we take each and every day and we will choose that path totally depending on what we need *emotionally, physically, spiritually or mentally.*

Our lives, or should I say path, are what we can tolerate.

Understanding the control you have in your Reality. I know...
it is easy for me to say that you can change your path
anytime you want to... You can, and that is a fact! But there
is a reason that you might not be able to... at this time. First,
you will need to understand the *Basic human needs of
survival* before you can enjoy your life and be on the path of
your choice. Even the worst of criminals have needs!

## Maslow's Hierarchy of needs

This drawing represents, in order of importance (1-5), the basic needs of a human being.

Questions to ask:

Where are you on your life path at the moment?
Which one of the five levels are you on?

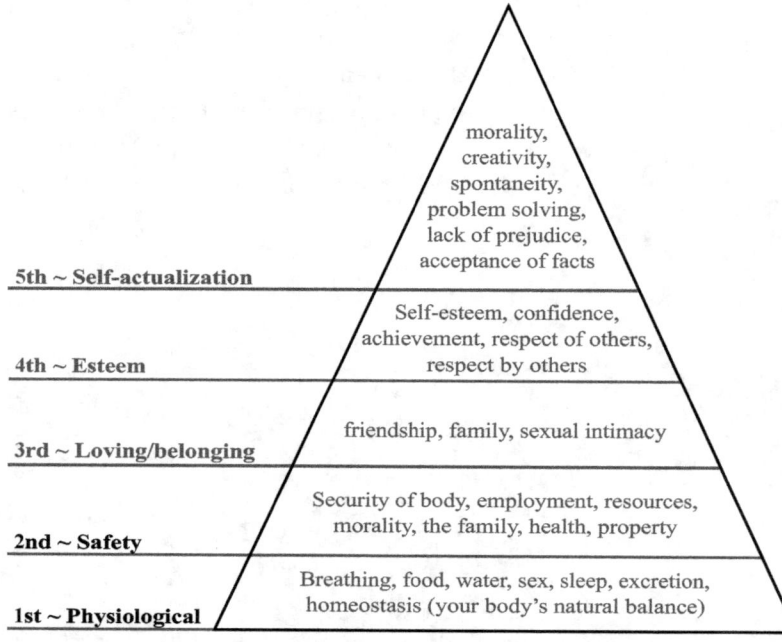

5th ~ Self-actualization — morality, creativity, spontaneity, problem solving, lack of prejudice, acceptance of facts

4th ~ Esteem — Self-esteem, confidence, achievement, respect of others, respect by others

3rd ~ Loving/belonging — friendship, family, sexual intimacy

2nd ~ Safety — Security of body, employment, resources, morality, the family, health, property

1st ~ Physiological — Breathing, food, water, sex, sleep, excretion, homeostasis (your body's natural balance)

- **1st is Physiological**
  The base of all human needs;
    - Breathing, food, water, sex, sleep, excretion, homeostasis (your body's natural balance)
- **2nd is Safety;**
    - Security of body, employment, resources, morality, the family, health, property.
- **3rd is Love/Belonging;**
    - Friendship, family, sexual intimacy
- **4th is Esteem;**
    - Self-esteem, confidence, achievement, respect of others, respect by others
- **5th is Self-actualization;**
    - Morality, creativity, spontaneity, problem solving, lack of prejudice, acceptance of facts

Fairy Tales, Dreams and Reality...

**Question...** Is it hard for you to dream about buying a beautiful big house when you cannot even buy enough food to put on the table? Of course, it would be.

You cannot help someone whose basic needs are not being met. This means a person cannot choose to change their path if their needs are not being met in order of Maslow's Hierarchy: physiological, safety, love/belonging, esteem, and self-actualization.

If you want to improve your self-esteem and you have nowhere to sleep, you will not be able to improve until you have a place to sleep.

Once you meet all your needs in the first level, you can work towards changing your path to the next level. If all your Physiological level needs are met, you can choose to change and make sure that your Safety level needs are met. Then, we move on to the Love & Belonging level, the Esteem level, and the Self-actualization level.

When your physiological and safety needs are met, you can proceed to improve other areas in your life, like:

- Family
- Health & Fitness
- Job or Career
- Personal Growth
- Relationships
- Spirituality

Most motivational books and seminars are taught to people already in the last two levels: Esteem and Self-actualization.

Throughout your lifetime, you may move up and down within all five levels, depending on your choices. You may have grown up in a beautiful house, had many friends, and never had to worry about money, and when you turned nineteen, you left home, got married, and had children. With each new experience, your path changed. Years later, your parents died, and your spouse left you with two children to bring up on your own, and worse yet, you have no job... Hey, it happens.

There are experiences in life that you will not be in control, and they could easily change your path; accidents, for example, are not always planned, but the experience can affect many peoples' lives at once. September 11, 2001, to give an example. Most of us would not have any idea that was going to happen. It affected many of us, some more than others. Was this accident planned? There are stories of people who were late to work that day and missed the United Airlines Flight 93 plane. Why did they get to live?

You mean sometimes accidents are planned…yes, maybe unconsciously, but yes. I have heard many people say that they were trying to get out of a job, relationship or school but could not because of the lack of money or because their parents would not let them. Well, an accident happens…and voilà, you are no longer at the job, relationship, or school.

You know that old saying.

> *Be careful what you wish or pray for… for you may just get it. Maybe it should be… unless you know what to do with it once you get it.*

No matter where you are on your path, tomorrow is another day, and the only thing you can count on (and it is a fact) is CHANGE all you can do is learn to adapt to the new experience and try to make the best of it or at least learn from the experience.

**So maybe the secret to a great path is mind over matter?**

## Body versus Mind

### I believe it is mind over matter!

Experiences will happen to you that will lead many of you to question what you believe and/or the path you choose to take.

One example of body vs mind: my son brought home a four-person chess game one day. He and I decided to play it alone since we didn't have four people to play. The game is set up like the two-player version except that the board is bigger and accommodates four players, one on each side of the square board. I played the silver player in front of me and gold directly across from me. He played the other two, white and black.

The game has the same rules and moves as the traditional version; one person moves, and then the other moves clockwise. All individual pieces can only move in the traditional patterns. The big difference is you have four sets of chess pieces on the board at one time instead of two, and you can kill any of the other three players, but if you are only playing with two players instead of four, then you seem only to want to kill the other person colors. We started the game as usual; the first player moves a game piece.

I started the game by moving one of my silver pieces. He moved a black piece; I moved gold, a white piece, and so forth around the board.

At first, there was nothing new to the game. We just kept moving the appropriate colored piece. After quite a few moves, it started to happen. I had a move that could conquer (kill) one of his pieces.

He abruptly said, "Mom, you can't do that; it's not that colors turn." He was correct. It wasn't. So, I moved the correct colored piece. No-kill, and then he took his turn.

My next move came, and I made my move for the next kill. Again, he said, as he shook his head and made a face like I was nuts, "Mom, wrong color." It took me by surprise that I had just made the same mistake.

I started writing down my color so I wouldn't make the mistake again.

It didn't help! I was still moving the wrong color to make the kill. So, I started to say the color out loud AND wrote it down…, but it didn't help. It took fourteen times, and I got a lot of weird looks from my son and words like 'Come on, what are you doing, or this is crazy' before I started to be able to move the correct colored piece.

After we were done with the game... of course, he won ...I called my husband on his cell phone (he was working a bit late) and told him what had just happened. I asked him to play our son when he got home to see his experience.

After my husband ate his dinner, he and our son started to play the four-person chess game. I was in the next room watching TV, so I couldn't influence the game. My husband already knew what happened to me and was sure he wouldn't make the same mistakes.

My husband and I had been playing chess for over twenty years, knew the rules, and were pretty good competitors for each other. Our son had started playing just a few years before and could already beat us.

About fifteen or twenty minutes into the game, I heard my husband's first "Sh...t". I smiled and another one a few minutes later. And our son said, "Dad, you are doing what Mom did." I could hear my husband fidget in his chair.

I said, "Told you it wasn't so easy."

Then, a few minutes later, he said, "This is a stupid game." Meaning he was moving the wrong-colored piece to make a kill.

Our son won that game, too.

Later, my husband said he would never play it again. And I replied, "It is just another game. We will just need to practice and learn it better." He never did play again. I did, though.

My son and I played it a couple more times, and each time, I was much better and learned not to make the mistake of moving the wrong-colored pieces.

I still remember how strange it was in the first game. I knew what color I was to move, but I got caught up in the kill and moved by instinct instead. My body just did it even though I was writing it down and saying it out loud.

What a feeling to be out of control, my mind wanting one thing and my body doing another.

It is the same for eating, sex, spending money, drugs, alcohol, travel, health, and so forth...our minds may know what the best thing to do is, but our bodies (maybe instincts/habits) seem to do another.

Fairy Tales, Dreams and Reality...

I also learned that 'practice makes (just about) perfect.' Our body is amazing; if you put your mind to something, you can achieve it!

Many of you will need to know the scientific details of how your body and mind work and contribute to your path choice.

### The Why and the How it works...

**Let's explore how the body and mind are connected.**

To truly be able to change, you should have a basic understanding of how your body creates your reality.

I split the Human body into two different categories Body controlled by the brain and the Mind:

**Anatomy and physiology of the Body:** Skeletal (bones), Muscular (muscles), Urinary (bathroom #1), Reproductive (sex organs), Endocrine (hormonal), Lymphatic (detox and removal), Immune (kill and detox), Digestive (what we eat, how it is used and exit #2), Cardiovascular (blood), Respiratory (breathing), Neurological (nervous) and special senses (touch, sight, sound, smell, and taste) systems.  And your **Mind** which is considered part of the brain (in the neurological system). The brain is the part that tells the rest of the body (other systems) what to do.
Without a brain, you would not be alive, and two (most importantly for this book), you would not be able to change your path.

You will need to understand the Nervous System's importance to understand why you do what you do.

**The Nervous System is composed of two major parts:**

1st  -  Central Nervous System (CNS) - brain and spinal column
    \*where memories are stored

   2nd -  Peripheral Nervous System (PNS) - sensory nerves (touch) and motor nerves (movement).

I would like you to take notice of the pathway from the CNS to the hippocampus and the pathway from the PNS to the ANS to the sympathetic and parasympathetic.

**Why are they important?**

The first one, CNS, is how you retain and recall your memories; the second, PNS, is how you respond to outside influences (fight and flight or rest and repair).

**1st The Central Nervous System (CNS)** - which consists of the Brain and Spinal Column, is considered the supervisor of the body's nervous activity.

In layperson's terms, if you are outside and it is a beautiful March morning in Kelowna, you went for a walk but did not bring a warm jacket because it seemed so nice when the sun was out. On the walk back, the clouds came, and a chilly light breeze blew across your face and arms. A moment or two later, your body would notice and respond to the chilly breeze that is moving past the hair on your face and arms, and you may start to shiver or rub your arms as a natural response of your body protecting itself from the cold.

Scientifically, this movement/stimulus sends a nerve impulse to the brain, and the brain sends an impulse/message to the muscles to shiver to stay warm.

A diagram for those of you who like to see the brain and the main three parts:

1. cerebrum (your conscious thought)

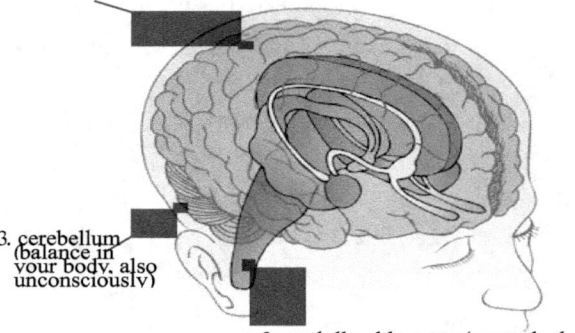

3. cerebellum (balance in your body, also unconsciously)

2. medulla oblongata (controls the unconscious parts of your body)

• The *cerebrum* is the largest area of the brain (take note of the arrow pointing to the area on top and notice the same texture all over). The cerebrum comprises the conscious brain and is divided into two hemispheres: the left (the analytical part of you) and the right (the creative part of you).

• Function: intelligence and reasoning, personality, interpretation of sensory impulses, motor function, planning and organization, memory, and touch sensation.

• The *medulla oblongata* is the part of the brain that connects to the spinal cord.

• Function: Medulla oblongata makes up the unconscious part of your brain, like regulating your heartbeat, breathing, blood pressure, vomiting, coughing, sneezing, swallowing, and hiccup ping.

• The *cerebellum* is the second largest part of the brain after the cerebrum. It is located just at the lower back portion of your skull.

• Function: muscle coordination and maintaining normal muscle tone and posture. The cerebellum coordinates balance.

**2nd The Peripheral Nervous System (PNS) -** is made up of sensory and motor nerves. These nerves extend from the brain and spinal cord and link to all other body parts (for example, your organs).

• **Somatic Nervous System (SNS) -** The somatic nervous system is responsible for voluntary control (you have conscious control and can make your body do something). Maybe you want to move to go get a glass of water. This part of the nervous system helps the muscles to move and tells you when you touch something too hot or cold.

• **Autonomic Nervous System (ANS) -** normally operates without voluntary control (it is unconscious, or we are unaware). For, when you climb stairs, your muscles are under conscious control and receive orders from the brain via the nerves of the PNS, but while you are walking up the stairs, can you tell me you are thinking what your pancreas, liver, or spleen is doing? No, those organs are working unconsciously in your body because the medulla oblongata told those organs what to do for you.

Fairy Tales, Dreams and Reality...

There are two major divisions in the ANS which are:

- **Sympathetic nerves - create fight and flight response**
- **Parasympathetic nerves - create rest and repair response**

These two, Sympathetic and Parasympathetic, are very important to know about because how you handle your outside influences determines how your body will respond and what path you will create for yourself.

You have two choices in any situation: Sympathetic (fight and/or flight) and Parasympathetic (rest and/or repair). You will always react more often to outside influences than to internal influences.

You will respond if you walk in the forest and a big bear crosses your path! You will either fight it and/or run...or you might faint and pray it thinks you are dead, and if it mauls you, you will need rest to repair in the hospital.

A basic example of a reaction to an outside influence is to imagine it is your first time seeing a cactus plant that has many prickly spines or scales on it, and you reach out to touch it...outside influence (something new to you) the plant which creates a reaction...you wanting to touch it. The brain wants to understand the cactus (the hand reaches out to touch it), and the body automatically reacts (the hand is instantly withdrawn) because of the pain when the finger touches the cactus's pointy spine.

Or you could imagine the first time a child sees a candle flame and reaches out to touch the flame. Correct your body has an unconscious reaction to stimuli, good or bad.

A baby is born with only two natural fears: loud sounds and the feeling of falling. Everything else is a memory taught to us by witnessing it, doing it, or having the fear drilled into us (meaning there is a worse punishment – grounded, beaten, etc.), which influences our choice of staying on our path or changing to another one.

Your brain needs to comprehend all experiences and will to decide how to react...and depending on the magnitude of the experience (good, bad, or blah) will determine if you keep it as a memory in your mind.

## Memory

Your bad memories, experiences, and path choices are why I, or any other practitioner in this field, have clients or students. I believe part of my job is to help you change a negative issue in your life to a positive one! Remember, these are just bad memories and are not set in stone for life in your brain. You can change your mind and decide to take another path anytime you choose to.

As long as your body does not have a physical issue due to drugs, alcohol, surgery, or hormones, you can change the emotional charge you have with any negative experience you remember that is holding you back from choosing a new path of your choice. If you do have a chemical imbalance or have had surgery, you will most likely be able to change your path. It just might take longer to change the emotional residue remaining.

For those of you who love knowledge and detail, here it is… more information on how the body stores these memories and exactly where in your brain. And for those of you that this is too much information, just skim through and read the sections that interest you.

Memory
•      The brain can store, retain, and subsequently retrieve information through our daily senses of touch, sight, smell, taste, and sound.
•      Memories are stored in the limbic system inside the brain's cerebrum. The main anatomical parts are the Hypothalamus, Amygdala, Hippocampus, and Thalamus.

In short, your experiences and emotions that you sense (good or bad) are taken in during the day by the Hypothalamus and are stored for the day in the Amygdala. When you sleep, the information of the day is sorted out in the Hippocampus (some say that is how your dreams are formed), the important (good or bad) memories are stored for retrieval, and the rest of the day's information is erased.

## Limbic System

As you can see, in the middle part of the brain are the three structures: the Hypothalamus, the Amygdala, and Hippocampus.

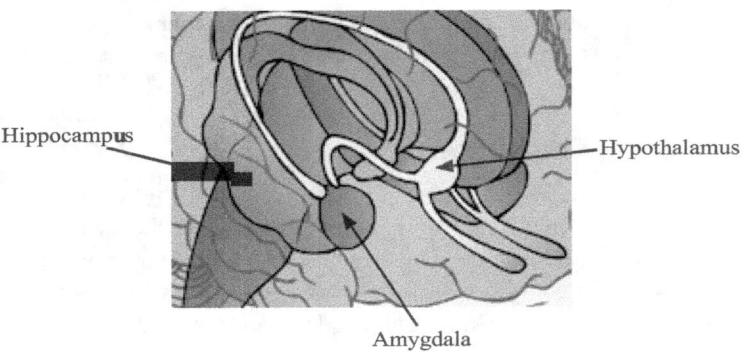

Hippocampus

Hypothalamus

Amygdala

*Hypothalamus* - It controls our motivated behaviors, like thermal regulation, sexuality, combativeness, hunger, and thirst.
It is believed to play a major role in our emotions, specifically pleasure and rage, aversion, displeasure, and a tendency to uncontrollable and loud laughing.

However, the hypothalamus has more to do with emotional expression (symptomatic –fight and flight). This means that when the physical symptoms of emotion appear (like wanting to cry in a public place but being too embarrassed if that happened), a past memory from childhood triggers the memory or fear in the hypothalamus (limbic system). It may create anxiety in the body, which triggers you to respond to this negative feedback, causing you to run (fight and flight) from the scene so you do not embarrass yourself again.

*Amygdala* - Deep inside the brain, a little almond-shaped structure connects with the hippocampus, the thalamus.
These connections make it possible for the amygdala to play its important role in mediating and controlling major affective activities like friendship, love, and affection, on the expression of mood, and mainly, fear, rage, and aggression, and can identify danger.

Humans with marked amygdala lesions lose the effective meaning of the perception of outside information, such as the recognition of a well-known person. The person knows precisely who the other person is but cannot decide whether he likes or dislikes him (or her).

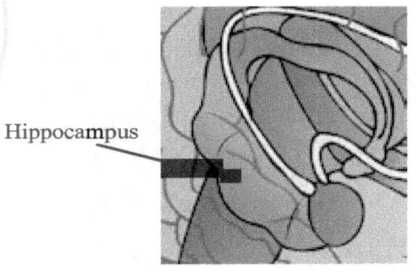

Hippocampus

*Hippocampus* -The Hippocampus is mainly involved with memory phenomena, especially forming long-term memory (which sometimes lasts forever). Nothing can be retained in the memory when both hippocampi (right and left) are destroyed. The subject quickly forgets any recently received message. An intact hippocampus allows a person to compare a present situation with a similar past experience(s), thus being able to choose the best option.

Thinking about why you need to know this in such detail. Not all of you will need to understand this information, but those of you who truly desire to change your path need to know how you ended up on that path and what is controlling you to stay on it.

### Types of Memory

There are two types of memories that you should know about. If you have not figured it out by now, these two memories control who you are and if you are consciously in control of your path!

**Long-term memory** can disappear by what is considered the natural forgetting process. To retain a memory for a long, long time, the thought or experience you want to remember would need to have made a major impact on you (good or bad), or you would have to do something repetitively, over and over again, so it becomes a habit to make the memory last for years.

Did you know that long-term memory can last as little as a few days or as long as decades?

**Short-term memory** holds a small amount of information for about 20 -30 seconds. The information held in short-term memory may be recently processed information or information recently retrieved from long-term memory.

**Working memory** is when you are consciously working on a project and are reading, writing, or talking about information that you may decide to keep as short- or long-term memory later.

**This is fascinating information on how your memories are stored.**

Scientists say that we only consciously retain about 9 bits of information (outside stimulus) every second; even that is still a lot of information the brain has to deal with. This daily information is stored in the amygdala during waking hours, and at night, when you sleep, this information gets sorted through. Information (good or bad) that the mind decides to keep goes to the hippocampus (long-term memory), and the information not needed is erased.

The best example of what your brain remembers is pleasure and pain. The more pleasurable or painful, the easier it is to remember. Most people remember things by association: smell, taste, sight, sound, or how something feels. All information in our memory is somehow associated with something.

> Think of an orange…color, texture, shape, smell, taste, fruit, and nutrients. You do not usually think of a big fat purple elephant when you think of orange unless there is some interesting story to go with it (I bet you now have a thought or image of a big fat purple elephant, though).

Most of us have a really good memory, but we do not have practice using it efficiently. There are courses taught on teaching memory with association. An example would be remembering someone's name when you meet them (say the name over three times while associating it with something). Or an acronym, ABC, most of us would instantly go to the Alphabet or H2O for water. Some of us remember words by sayings. I had a hard time remembering how to spell together when I was young and taught myself to remember by saying to myself to-get-her. I would see getting a girl. Or maybe the word Island (is- land).

Two things must also happen for you to remember something easily:
• 1st, you need to be in the **'same state of awareness'** (the body and mind are feeling the same awareness of the surroundings as it was at another time). Imagine you arrive home from work exhausted and hungry, carrying bags or paperwork, telling the kids to go do their homework, and tripping over the dog while kicking off your

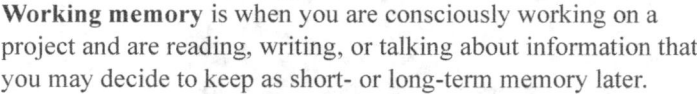

Fairy Tales, Dreams and Reality...

shoes. It is no wonder that your keys are missing the following day. In the morning, you are in a different state of consciousness (usually refreshed and ready to go… unless you didn't get your coffee – another memory stimulus – caffeine and habit) than the night before (tired and doing too many things at once).

• 2nd, you need a destination/location for your keys, regardless of state. Be it your purse, tabletop, key hanger, etc. (association). You can improve your memory by forming associations or creating a new habit with what is important to you. A habit takes 21-42 days to form or break and sometimes needs to be refreshed months later (depending on how long the habit has been practiced in the past).

Another interesting tidbit is that there is a belief that when you die, you can only take your memories with you because the physical brain dies, and so the ability to think is gone. So, your mind goes to heaven, but your ability to experience or contemplate anything dies here on earth.

**What it comes down to is…**

Most of us are given praise when we do something good and punished when we do something bad, and we remember or store only the very good or bad memories in our brain's limbic system. The boring or same old, same old memories just disappear since the mind only has the energy to remember so much information and seems always to choose the really, really good or the really, really bad.

You will only change your path or beliefs when:

• You have realized there is a better way

• If the masses are doing it

• The bad habit becomes destructive

• Life gets so bad that you will do anything to change it Each and every day, you have to choose to notice an issue and decide to change the feelings that are controlling you to make that decision. Hopefully, by this part of the book, you know you have the power to change your mind!

Your mind is considered very different from your brain…

**The Mind is considered to be inside of the brain.**
* Mind: the element of a person that enables them to be aware of the world and their experiences, to think and to feel; the faculty of consciousness and thought. **Three parts make up the mind:** conscious, subconscious, and superconscious.

**Conscious Mind** (most of us think we are in control of our lives)
* The state of being aware of and responsive to one's surroundings.

* Stored in the amygdale (limbic system)

* Acts as a filter for thought or outside influences.

* Thinks or analyzes information

* Controls our movements

* Responsibilities

* 7 to 9,000,000,000.00 bits of information every second. We only consciously notice about 9 bits.

* In seconds (response time):
  From sight to touch ….............. 0.071
  From touch to sight. ….............. 0.053
  From sight to hearing …............0.16
  From hearing to sight …............0.06
  From one ear to another …..........0.064

**Subconscious** (is the part of you that really controls your life)
* Of or concerning the part of the mind of which one is not fully aware but which influences one's actions and feelings.

* Stored in the hippocampus (limbic system)

* Stores your belief system, self-image, morals, habits, emotions, fears, secrets, and memories

* Cannot tell the difference between real and imagined

* Understands subliminal messages

* Ability to solve problems creatively

* Dreams

* Some believe Psychic ability is accessed here

**Superconscious** (the part of you that God sends messages to)
* Transcending human or normal consciousness (Higher power)

* Higher self.

* Accessible through meditation, yoga, breathing, and hypnosis

* Group consciousness or God consciousness

- Healing
- All-knowing, higher power
- Akasha records (spiritual knowledge of past, present, and future events) can be obtained.
- Brilliant ideas, music, art, movies, stories, and concepts are formatted here- Einstein, Nostradamus, etc.

The mind is what makes us who we are and our beliefs; judgments of pleasure and pain dictate our next move.

**Do you really get it?**

Now that you read about how the brain works and what part of the brain is in control of your path choice, I am still not sure if you get the picture.

One minute, everything is going good, and all of a sudden, the world seems like it turned upside down.

Sometimes, our path changes, and we do not understand the reason until days, months, or even years later, and we look back and think, 'I am so glad that happened.' One example is a relationship that did not work out; one person left, and the other is heartbroken and very upset. But years later, the heartbroken person looks back and understands that what he/ she has now is way better than the path he/she would have been on if he/she had still been with that person.

Usually, the news in other places of the world does not affect us very much, and unless you have an immediate relationship to the situation, you will not react. If we have never lived through anything similar to a horrendous destruction from weather, famine, or war, it will just seem like a fairy tale to many of us. And we will go on living our lives like nothing has happened. If we did not have worldwide news coverage, we would not even know any problems or issues anywhere else on the planet.

And then, every so often, something happens that can affect many nations all at once.

*Good or Bad...*

- On December 31st, 1999, I remember going to the grocery store in a bit of a panic mode due to the media dictating the doom day of life, all because of a belief that the computers would not work at 12:01 am on January 01/2000. I remember trying to think that it would be okay, but my body was in panic mode. I had gone into the grocery store and prayed to God to tell me what to buy. By the time I was at the till, I only had a couple of items in the cart. As I was leaving, I paid for the items and asked God why I felt this way if there was no real problem. The answer was I was feeling other people's panic around me.

-       In August of 2008, life seemed normal. People in Canada were buying homes, furniture, and toys, building new businesses, going on trips, and planning their retirement…life was good. Most Canadians did not realize that the US marketplace had been going downward for a few years and that the US economy could affect us. Even though previously there were signs that change was going to happen, examples are 9/11 and the forestry industry going on a downslide.

The economic situation in 2008 left many older people realizing that they would never be able to make up the money they had just lost in the stock market crash and would have to change their lifestyle.

-       The media can play a big part in the reaction and emotions of what people believe and feel. When TV newscasters or newspaper editors blaze their version of the stock market crash with the gloom about it, the people's reaction is panic. People sell out on their declining stock values, try to save themselves, and start to think anything is better than nothing.

Even though professional economists have been tracking cycles and patterns in the global economy for years, they could tell that something negative was bound to happen due to the number of baby boomers retiring soon. The crash just happened a little sooner than they had predicted. All this happened while most of us were in our own bubble of life and did not pay any attention to that information.

Do you think you would have believed the professional economists? Would you have chosen a different path for your finances? When most people do not have any proof that the money/stock market would go down or fall, and at that moment in time, they had evidence of the stock market still going up, and their thought and desire to make more money was the intent.

Most people would not have cashed out in advance. It's like a person at a poker table who has contributed some money to the game and won a bit but has the mindset to win even more. That fact is that most people lose all the money they started with before leaving the poker table (think about it: how a casino makes money).

All information of history is, as one person remembers it to be… from the witness's point of view. Depending on the perspective, the interpretation can be very different from one person to the next. Perspective from behind the person, beside the person, across the street, or maybe a bird's eye view (above the person) will be very different. What if the person blinked or had a personal interest in the accident, meaning something similar happened to him?

Another example is this book; it is based on my perspective, and you are reading it from your perspective, which will be different than a friend's perspective reading this book.

For example, history has been rewritten a few times that the Earth is flat. We know today it is not, that it is round. How many planets are in our Solar system…nine? In 2005, Eris was founded, and in 2006, Ceres was named a dwarf planet. Now, there are eleven, and some say twelve if you include Nibiru. The bible recites many historic events that happened a thousand years ago; similar events are still happening today: famine, prostitution, war, hierarchy, etc.

The problem is that some still have old beliefs and have not adapted to the times. Many still find it hard to believe that there is an African American as President. Barack Obama had a Global impact that affected many of us… so many people (of all cultures and ethnic groups) were extremely happy that a young African American was elected for President of the United States of America…proof that dreams can come true, and history can be changed.

**I believe he represents what most of us forget:** To keep living our dreams, to have a vision or feeling or thought or words and think for ourselves… and change our path for the better.

Now, I want you to imagine that you are a buffalo grazing in a meadow in the middle of a large herd, and all of a sudden, many of the other buffalos start running… do you ask what is happening and if you should follow them …no, more than likely you will just follow the masses and begin to run with them even if it is to your death over a cliff.

Most of us do not have enough factual information to really make an educated decision. So, we just react to the outside influences. We might speak our minds on a topic and believe what we are saying on the subject to be true, but did we study the information (all views or perspectives) ourselves, or did we just hear it and now believe it?

**To really understand something, you need to imagine you are the other person…**

**And that you are walking in their shoes.**

*Take note of all the sides of the situation.*

Our reactions create a memory in our brain and a neurological pattern that we keep following. Sometimes it is passed down from generation to generation…called patterns.

*There is a joke about a young married couple eating dinner, and the husband says to his wife, 'Why do you cut the ends off the roast?' She replies, 'Because that is how you cook roast. My mother cooks her roast that way, and my grandmother taught her how to cook roast that way.'*

*One Sunday, the whole family was gathered at the wife's mother's home for a roast dinner. The family was gathered at the table as the roast was being brought out from the kitchen. The young husband asks at the dinner table, 'Why do you cut the ends off the roast?' the mother answers, 'Well, of course, it is because that is how you cook a roast.' A moment later, the grandmother says, 'When I was first married, the pan I had and still have could only hold a roast so big, so I had to cut the ends off of it so it could fit into the pan for cooking.*

Here is another tidbit of information for you to think about:

Did you know that some say the government formed the English alphabet to be able to create a certain type of society and taught us to write and print it in a very precise and strict way for a reason? Upper- and lower-case letters were to be formed in a special size, form, and slant/angle that all had to be followed perfectly, and a left-handed person was punished for not using their correct hand, which is the right one.

Graphology (handwriting analogy) studies how people create their letters and how professionals can determine your personality, which could be used in hiring you for a specific job or used in the military or bank for a similar reason.

Many of us were taught:

- To do as we were told and/or shown.
- To never speak back or to ask any questions.
- Respect our Elders.

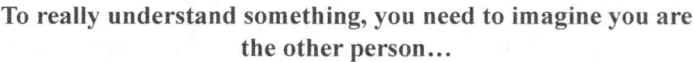

Fairy Tales, Dreams and Reality…

Starting from a newborn baby, we learn by listening, seeing, doing, and practicing or copying. As babies, we like and will repeat things that have a positive response: clapping, happy, excited voice, food, hugs, etc., and we will deter from any negative response: being hit or slapped, loud, angry voice, being sent to bed without supper, and being ignored. All these negative feelings are stored in our memories, controlling our choice of path in life.

**Where are you on your path...** Anyone stressed?
**Stress**

Stress has a major impact on your choice of path direction.

**Definition**
Stress has many definitions, but in this course, we will define stress as:
•      The sum of the biological reactions to any adverse stimulus, physical, mental, or emotional, internal or external, disturbs an organism's homeostasis.

**Stress Categories**
Stress can be broken down into several categories. They are:
•      Physical
•      Mental
•      Emotional

**Physical Stress** - There are many types of physical stress, but they all fall into two main groups:
•      Emergency Stress - a situation that poses an immediate physical threat.
•      Continuing Stress - a situation caused by changes in the body by pregnancy, menopause, acute and chronic disease, continuing exposure to excessive noise, vibration, fumes, chemicals, or other agents.

**Mental Stress** - Mental stress comes into play with any imagined or real threat to the body. Some are classified as psychosomatic. Mental stress can also be divided into two types:
•      Emergency Stress - This comes into action when a person merely foresees or imagines danger as well as real emergencies.

• Continuing Stress - This is created by a person undergoing severe mental pressure in excess of forty-eight hours. It may be in combination with physical or emotional stress or on its own. It may be real or imagined. The causes are widely variable.

**Emotional Stress** – This may result from a self-image problem, a lifetime of negative experiences, the sudden shock of an emotional impact, or even a mental or physical condition or perception. It is perhaps the most dangerous and invasive of all the types of stress. Physical or mental stress is more likely to develop from emotional stress than the opposite. Emotional stress is considered continual.

*General-Adaption Syndrome (GAS)*

Physiologist Hans Selye introduced the term general-adaption syndrome to describe the body's response to stress. The response has three phases:

1. Alarm reaction. The adrenal medulla prepares the body for fight or flight.
2. Resistance Reaction. If stress continues for an extended period, the body enters the second stage. Blood pressure remains abnormally high during this stage, and metabolism speeds up. Protein breakdown is characteristic of this stage. Levels of hormones, including cortisol, aldosterone, thyroxine, and HGH are elevated.
3. Exhaustion Stage. The body wears out, and death can occur. Stress is a response by the body to protect itself. We undergo physiological changes that protect the body from harm in response to all stress. In our society and lifestyle, this response can be triggered more frequently. Often for reasons rarely experienced in the past. Work, the fast pace of our lives, and the impact of over 500 chemicals now found in our bodies that never existed 100 years ago are just examples of how we can be affected.

Many people believe that the stressful nature of our lives causes many persons to continuously remain in the resistance stage of GAS. Chronic stress is harmful because of the side effects of long-term elevated levels of cortisol. Glucocorticoids help reduce inflammation but also interfere with normal immune responses, so infections spread. Chronic high blood pressure can result in heart disease. Ulcers, high blood pressure, atherosclerosis, and arthritis are all linked to excessive hormone levels caused by stress.

Stress is a beneficial condition when it works to prevent harm. Stress can be considered a murderer when it gets out of control and continuous.

The adrenal medulla sets off an emergency stress response. The medulla of each adrenal gland is directly connected to the nervous system. When a crisis occurs, it pours the hormone epinephrine into the bloodstream. This:

- Dilates blood vessels
- Dilates pupils of the eyes • Raises blood pressure
- Raises blood sugar levels
- Speeds up the heart
- Slows production of mucous
- Slows or stops healing processes

A continual stress response is under the control of the adrenal glands. After the initial body reaction, the glands continue to produce a steady supply of hormones that increase the body's resistance. This is in addition to specific responses such as increased production of antibodies to fight infection. If the stress is overwhelming, the adrenal glands can be exhausted.

Psychological situations result in the same bodily response in the short term and spikes during the long term. However, the body adjusts to the continual state of stress, and the person may believe they are handling it well. The reactions have settled into a long, steady, high state of preparation, and the body starts to wear out.

It is very important to understand that:

- The perception of fear is a perception by the Autonomic Nervous System (ANS) that there is a threat. The individual consciousness may not be aware of a threat. Stage fright is a good example. The mind and emotions perceive a threat, but the conscious knows no danger exists.

- Each type of personality has its own stress response, internally and externally. They vary in degree and response time but will all react in the same steps in an emergency. However, over the long term, the body demonstrates a marked difference.

- Stress triggers an auto-immune malfunction, which cannot be corrected by normal medication. Stress causes an elevated leucocyte response, which can suppress the immune response.

- Organs such as the liver, pancreas, adrenals, and kidneys alter function due to excessive or prolonged stress. In essence, they function poorly.

- The lymphatic system can be stimulated to override the auto-immune. This results in an increase in lymphocytes and a corresponding decrease in leucocytes.

- Sudden or excessive exercise causes a stress response in the muscular and lymphatic systems. They struggle to cope with the threat and response.

It is important to understand that you can do something about stress. You must act to:

- Lessen the perception of stress or threat. Helping you change your outlook on the cause of your stress.

- Calm and uplift the hypothalamus. It plays a major role in the control of the auto-immune system.

- Do not use essential oils that stimulate the auto-immune. Use essential oils that calm or slow the system and its response.

- Recognize what may be stress-related. Many diseases and illnesses result from stress. Among them are diabetes, Crohn's, arthritis, IBS, Sjogren's syndrome, Raynaud's, lupus, fibromyalgia, chronic fatigue syndrome, eczema, psoriasis, alopecia, insomnia, irritability, muscle spasms, kidney disease, respiratory problems, celiac, and allergies.

- Treatment must take a long-term approach. There is no short-term cure.

Many symptoms are common to other conditions but may have unique triggers with auto-immune or stress diseases. Things such as fluid retention, joint pain, lack of sexual interest, and irritability all reflect stress.

Although stress conditions are not usually considered life-threatening, just life-quality destruction, a more realistic picture is emerging. Heart attacks, strokes, etc., can and often kill or seriously maim.

Finally, the changing social conditions, years of age, and weather all play a role in stress response. You can witness growing reactions as the population increases. Crowds and lineups all cause a body response to speed up. During certain weather patterns (high pressure), people are irritated more and respond faster. As you age, your youthful and laid-back approach changes. This is often a response to mental aging but can reflect the changing hormones in your body. It is recognized that women undergo a major change in life and hormones, and this can explain many of their responses.

Less understood is the fact that men also undergo a dramatic change that can seriously affect their quality of life, self-esteem, and their response to stress.

**Stress Reactions:**
Possible resulting conditions;

- Allergies • Insomnia
- Alopecia • Irritable bowel syndrome
- Arthritis • Irritability
- Celiac • Kidney Disease
- Chronic Fatigue • Muscle Spasms
- Crohn's • Lupus
- Diabetes • Psoriasis
- Eczema • Raynard's
- Fibromyalgia • Respiratory problems

**Stress Conclusion**
Never underestimate the threat posed by stress and the power of stress or its ability to go unrecognized. Many people fail to recognize stress or the effect it has on them. You must tune into your body, be aware, and take notice. It is almost always your number one condition and frequently the cause of many issues or health problems encountered in one's life.

**Holmes and Rabe Social Readjustment Rating Scale**
There are many pressures in your life, and a chart of stressors has been developed and used for several years to help determine your stress level. The chart is the "Holmes and Rabe Social Readjustment Rating Scale."

You use the scale to determine how stressed you are. Simply add the numbers for selected events in your life, and you can immediately get some relatively accurate guidance. An arbitrary number of 100 was given to the death of a partner. Other events were measured in relation to that event. A rating of 150 is estimated to be associated with a fifty (50) percent chance of a major health breakdown. A score of 300 or more has an eighty (80) percent chance during the following two years. Fewer than 100 are desirable, but only a few manage that rating. If under 100, you are considered to have no increased risk due to stress.

The ten most stressful events are almost all connected to a loss. They are:

- Being fired
- Death of a partner
- Divorce
- Imprisonment
- Marriage

- Marital separation
- Marital reconciliation
- Pregnancy
- Retirement
- Serious personal injury or illness

The following table outlines the value given to each stressful event:

| Event | Value |
|---|---|
| Death of a Partner | 100 |
| Divorce | 73 |
| Separation from a partner | 65 |
| Jail Sentence | 63 |
| Death of a close family member | 63 |
| Injury or illness to yourself | 53 |
| Marriage-your own | 50 |
| Fired at work | 47 |
| Reconciliation with a partner. | 45 |
| Retirement | 45 |
| Ill Health-member of your family | 44 |
| Pregnancy-your own | 40 |
| Sexual problems/difficulties | 39 |
| Major business or work change | 39 |
| Addition of a new family member. | 39 |
| Child leaves home | 39 |
| Change in your financial state | 38 |
| Death of a friend. | 37 |
| Change to a different type of work | 36 |
| More arguments with your partner | 35 |
| Take on a large mortgage | 31 |
| Mortgage or loan foreclosed | 30 |
| Change in responsibilities at work. | 29 |
| Trouble with in-laws | 29 |
| Outstanding personal achievement | 28 |
| Wife begins or stops work | 26 |
| Child begins or ends school | 26 |
| Change in living conditions | 25 |
| Change of personal habits | 24 |
| Trouble with the boss or employer | 23 |
| Change working hours or conditions | 20 |
| Change in residence | 20 |

Child changes schools. . . . . . . . . 20
Change in church activities. . . . . . . 19
Change in social activities . . . . . . . 18
Change in sleeping habits. . . . . . . . 16
Change in # of family gatherings  . . . . 15
Change in eating habits . . . . . . . . . 15
Holiday . . . . . . . . . . . . . . . . . 13
Christmas (coming soon) . . . . . . . . .12
Minor violations of the law. . . . . . . . 11

*Pleasure and pain (good or bad experiences) control your path choice and direction.*

Healing your stress is one of the best ways to be on a great path and a great life!

### Healing Stress
What will you do to get rid of the stress in your life?

Every time you are reminded or think about your health or a life problem/issue, you are stressing the body, and the body will constantly move from a parasympathetic (rest and relaxed) state to a sympathetic  (flight and fight) state with negative thoughts. Over time, this stress can cause physical trauma to the mind or body, and you may need counseling, medicine, surgery and/or drugs to try to fix the issue that the stress has caused you.

The goal in supporting modern medicine or any other therapy is that you need to receive and understand the lesson you are being given; the origin of the issue is usually where to start, and with it, you can heal stress and many other ailments that are caused by stress so you may remain in the parasympathetic state and fact, heal your body.

Although this may at first be perceived as of less importance to reduce the stress, the impact on you will be great. Effectively reducing stress, even for short periods, by learning a method to control your stress throughout the day will allow you to develop an active role in your health care. The belief that he/she is involved and starts to feel better Emotionally, Physically, Spiritually, and Mentally will greatly aid the whole healing process.

I have had a couple of experiences being involved in healing with my grandmother. One time, she was having pain and trouble walking with her hip and leg. I did not hear about it right away, and after a few weeks, she told me a friend of hers said, 'Doesn't your granddaughter do alternative healing?' So she called me and came in for a session. I start by doing Reflexology; this treatment is very good for someone not into alternative medicine. Because the client keeps their clothes on and is usually sitting and can watch what you are doing, it seems to give them the control they need, and they start to relax and bring themselves into a parasympathetic state. Of course, Reflexology creates circulatory and lymphatic movement, which helps clean and stimulate the body for homeostasis (balance).

While working on her feet, I started to get these images of her doing too much, which was her way of not having to say 'no' to anyone. We started to talk about everything she was doing in her week: cooking dinner for family members, playing bridge, volunteering at the hospital, church, and a few other things. I asked if she liked the pain and not being able to walk, just to have an excuse to be able to say no when someone asked her to help out when she really did not feel like it.

She healed within a few days of our session and also was able to slow down a bit, at least to her comfort level, and has not had any relapse for many years.

Stress can cause many symptoms and issues, and we do not always think to ask, 'Why am I having this issue?'

Another time, my grandmother went to the doctor due to intense pain in her forehead. She thought coincidentally that it might have been caused when she hugged someone, and their eyeglasses had caught and gave her a small cut that did not bleed. Her doctor said it was not possible that the little cut could cause the headache, and it was nothing to go home and take an aspirin. She said he made her feel like she was neurotic.

It hurt even worse the next day, and she went to a walk-in clinic. And that the doctor diagnosed it as Shingles and that if she had been."

Even a day earlier, he could have given her some medication to stop it from getting worse. As the days went on, her sore became very infected and spread. Within a few days, it looked like she had been in a motorcycle accident, and the left side of her face had major road rash.

The doctor had given her medication to deal with the condition and pain, and she became even sicker. She went back to see her doctor but had to see his replacement because he had gone on vacation, and the new doctor would not take her off the medication.

Even though she now had family around twenty-four-seven looking after her, I went over every day to see what I could do. I made an aromatherapy blend and did foot reflexology and Reiki on her while there. To this day, she still says that is what helped her make it through; the pain relief while I was working on her gave her a couple of hours with little pain, and she could rest.

After a couple of weeks of this pain, she was going downhill fast, and I told my mom, "She will die. You have to do something." She was pretty much bedridden and felt faint and was sick often even though she was not eating hardly anything. She looked like she aged twenty years in two weeks. My Aunt and cousin took her to the emergency at the hospital, and there, the doctors took her off of the medication, gave her a salt drip through intravenous, and made her drink a potassium drink every few hours. Within a few hours, she had gone from death's bed to almost back to normal. It was amazing to witness the transformation of healing. It seemed she was allergic to the medication the first doctor prescribed for her.

I find it interesting how a person can have a choice to live or die, be sick or heal, and be the catalyst for outside world change. My family all love my grandmother very much, and she must have needed a reminder of just how much and we needed a reminder that we still love and need her here.

Note to self:

- Always check the medication first! It might be killing you with a negative side effect.
- The Hospital emergency doctors can overrule any other doctor's orders.
- There is always a lesson in the negative experience.

I have had a few issues myself: a birthmark removed when I was three due to it being one that the doctors say could become cancerous. I had an eye operation at the age of eleven (almost twelve) due to an accident when I was one and a half and a tailbone operation when I was seventeen due to falling off a horse when I was twelve.

My most recent was needing a hysterectomy. In 2005, during a routine pap test, my doctor told me it seems I had fibroids, and I was sent to a gynecologist for an ultrasound. It turned out I did. A couple of years later, I started... Taking care of your health and exploring different options when dealing with medical issues is important. Here's the continuation of your text with formatting for better readability:

For four years, I tried all kinds of alternative medicine: Aromatherapy, acupressure, meditation, hypnotherapy, spiritual release, energy work, herbs, counseling, and probably a few more modalities to try to heal my uterus. I finally gave in and requested the operation, which took eighteen months to receive. After the operation, I found out it was both fibroids and endometriosis, which had wrapped itself around my descending colon (large intestine) and left ovary. So, in the end, it was a very good thing I had the operation. There is no cure for endometriosis, and it can get much worse and cause major damage to the rest of the body.

Doctors do not know what causes fibroids; I think my uterus was damaged during the delivery of my youngest child (which is a story in itself). I feel I have dealt with my childhood issues, and this was my body's way of finalizing its healing.

If you are injured, the body cannot always heal the original damage and has to find an alternate way to balance (homeostasis) itself.

Most issues are caused by past trauma: Emotional, Mental, Spiritual, and Physical.

Do not forget modern medicine is an answer; alternative medicine is us looking after our bodies before it gets to a point where modern medicine has to take over to heal.

It's essential to prioritize your health and well-being; sometimes, a combination of conventional and alternative approaches can provide the best path to healing.

**How do you heal stress?**

There are many ways to accomplish this. Check mark the ones you do already.

Here are a few ideas (as long as they do not cause more stress):
- A holiday, long or short
- Aromatherapy
- Bach Remedy (flower essence)
- Biking
- Buy a puppy or goldfish
- Carry around or sleep by gemstones or crystals
- Change furniture around in a room.
- Counselling
- Creating any type
- Day at the spa: Manicure, Facial
- Fitness class, Yoga, Tai chi
- Gardening
- Go for a scenic drive
- Go for a walk, run, or dancing
- Go on a date
- Go swimming or sit in a hot tub or bath
- Go to a movie or watch TV
- Good food (know your limit)
- Groups / Clubs / Chamber of Commerce
- Horseback riding
- Hypnosis
- Listen to new music
- Meditation
- Massage, Shiatsu, acupressure, acupuncture, etc.
- New hair cut
- Paint or draw (any modality of art creation)
- Play a game
- Read a book
- Sit by trees or water or even a nursery store
- Skiing or Snowboarding
- Sleep or nap
- Shopping / buying new clothes (as long as there is extra money for it)
- Talk to a friend

Fairy Tales, Dreams and Reality...

- Take a course
- Tanning (safely) / the sun
- Time heals many things (it just might take time; an operation will take some time to heal).
- Visit friends and family
- Plus, many more…

**Resources for more serious stress issues:**
> Check-in your phone book:
>> Emotional Stress:

- Councillor / Psychiatrist
- Bach Remedy / Flower Essences
- Hypnotherapist / Meditation

Mental Stress:

- More education; Schools / College /Universities
- Learning centers: Sylvan Learning / Tutor
- A holiday/trip
- Meditation
- Balance your life with some physical exercise

Physical Stress:

- Physician / Doctor / Naturopath
- Health Practitioner
  Day Spa / Massage / Reflexology / ETC.
  Acupuncturist
  Herbologist
  Homeopathy

Spiritual Stress:
- Medium / Psychic
- Priest / Minister

Books, the internet, and seminars are also great ways to learn how to release your stress.

Learning your area's social expectations will also help lessen your stress level…

Many people have never learned what society expects, etiquette, or how to act in public.

Many of you find it silly of me to put in this book, but I have to. What if, just in case, one person needs to read this to understand? It would make life so much easier for so many.

### Social Expectations

### Etiquette

Etiquette: the rules of standard behavior in polite society.
• In society, there is a code or expectation for our social behavior (manners in speech, writing, dress, and behavior). Each society, social class, or groups (no matter what country they are from) have norms (standards) of diplomatic behavior that are expected.

Usually unwritten and expected but not always taught, we are just supposed to know what is expected. Unfortunately, many of us learn by copying our parents, who usually have never had lessons either.

Etiquette may reflect an underlying ethical code, or it may grow more as a fad or trend. In the eighteenth century in Britain, there was a peculiar fascination with seemingly trivial actions, such as the delicate manner in which a teacup was held, with the baby finger often gracefully elevated. These seemingly inconsequential gestures were significant markers of one's upper-class status.

Like "culture," it is a word that has gradually grown plural, especially in a multi-ethnic society with many clashing expectations. Thus, it is now possible to refer to "etiquette" or "a culture," realizing that these may not be universal.

Culture: The arts, humanities, literature, music, painting, philosophy, and the performing arts.

**Etiquette Norms**

Etiquette promotes how people interact with each other by conforming to the norms of society. Examples:

- Arrive promptly when expected
- Avoid disturbing others with unnecessary noise
- Comfort the bereaved
- Contribute to conversations without dominating them
- Eat neatly and quietly
- Follow the established rules of an organization upon becoming a member
- Greet relatives, friends, and acquaintances with warmth and respect
- Offer hospitality equally and generously to guests
- Offer assistance to those in need
- Refrain from insults and prying curiosity
- Respond to invitations promptly
- Wear clothing suited to the occasion

In upper-class Roman society, etiquette would have instructed a man to greet friends and acquaintances with decorum, according to their rank, refrain from showing emotions in public, keep his womenfolk secluded from his clients, support his family's position with public munificence (lavish in giving), etc. Meanwhile, middle- and lower-class societies conformed to different rules.

One can reasonably view etiquette as the minimal politics required to avoid major conflict in polite society and, as such, an important aspect of applied ethics. What is excellent etiquette in one society may be shocking in another.

**Manners**

Manners: a way of doing something, social behavior with respect to standards.

- In China, a person who takes the last item of food from a common plate or bowl without first offering it to others at the table may be seen as a glutton and insulting to the host's generosity.
- In most European cultures, a guest is expected to eat all of the food given to them as a compliment to the cooking quality.
- Confucius included rules for eating and speaking and his more philosophical sayings.

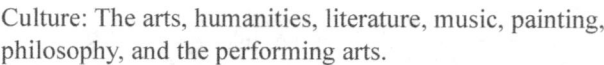

'Etiquette for Girls' and 'Manners for Men' guide those who want to combine a modern lifestyle with traditional values.

• Benjamin Franklin and George Washington wrote codes of conduct for young gentlemen in the American colonies.

• The immense popularity of advice columns and books by Letitia Baldrige and Miss Manners shows the currency of this topic.

• Even more recently, the rise of the Internet has necessitated the adaptation of existing rules of conduct to create Netiquette, which governs the drafting of email, rules for participating in an online forum, and so on.

• In Germany, there is an "unofficial" code of conduct called the Knigge, a book of high rules of conduct written by Adolph Freiherr Knigge in the late 18th century entitled exactly, Über den Umgang mit Menschen (On Human Relations). The code of conduct is still highly respected in Germany today and is used primarily in the higher society.

### Business Etiquette

**Business etiquette** is for social interaction to run more smoothly and applies to all levels of hierarchy, management, and staff interaction (even though there will be an expectation of respect between the two groups).

• Issues include cubicle life, usage of common areas, meetings, and other forms of social interaction within a work setting.

• Larger organizations tend to have stricter, expressly written rules on etiquette.

*If you have not gone to Miss Daisy's Etiquette school (Connie's imaginary school) for young boys and girls, hopefully, you have just lucked out having good common sense. If not, then here is what is expected.*

### Common Sense

Common Sense: Good sense, sound judgment in practical matters, common natural understanding, the knowledge, intuition, and experience that most people believe that they do or should have.

Common Sense is expected but not always taught.
Check mark the ones you do naturally or that you learned and still do:

Dinner Manners
• A host or hostess always serves themselves last

After a big meal, wait thirty minutes before swimming-your digestion needs time

- Ask to be excused from the table, but do not ever leave one person alone eating. Bring a gift if going to someone's home for dinner (unless it is your Mom and she would never expect a gift, you could always surprise her)
- Do not start until everyone is served (at least wait for the hostess)
- Eat with your mouth closed
- Eat with elbows off the table
- Eat slowly enough that everyone finishes at the same time
- Help or at least offer with clean up and dishes when at a friends or family for a meal
- If drinking alcohol, bring your own or drink only a glass or two
- Layout and use the proper table setting
- Most North Americans do not find burping polite
- No elbows on the table
- Taste before you swallow
- Wait for everyone to finish eating before leaving the table
- Watch how far out your elbows go when you cut your food
- Wipe your mouth on a napkin, not a sleeve
- When cooking food, do not leave and get distracted, for example, by the TV
- When finished eating, leave your fork and knife together (facing 11:00 o`clock)
- When at a restaurant, wait to walk out with the person paying the bill.
- Thank your hostess or person who made the dinner

Driving Manners

- Afraid of Semi trucks or bridges
- Are you used to driving in a big city or maybe a small city
- Do not assume everyone can drive the same
- Do not do drugs or drink and drive
- Check your vehicle tires and fluids for safe driving
- Clean your auto inside daily and wash, dust, and vacuum at least twice a year (spring and fall)
- Eyesight can be near or far.
- Eyesight can change at different times of the day.
- The height of the vehicle will make a big difference

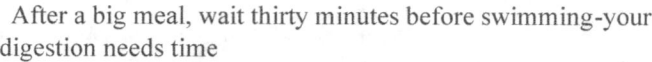

- He/she might be carrying something very breakable

'L' driver...give he/she room and your patience (it may just be his/her very first day, and an accident will take much more of your time)

- Let someone in when traffic is busy
- Let the city bus go ahead of you
- Let other cars onto the street ahead of you
- Might have just had an operation or accident and is being cautious
- 'N' drivers are of all ages and can be better drivers than you are; he/she has more laws to follow.
- Never give the keys to an automobile to a child
- New in town (maybe a tourist, do not forget they bring your town/city a lot of money)
- Speed of acceleration
- Turn your vehicle music down (bass especially) when you are in a neighborhood, at a stop sign, or at a red light
- Use winter tires in snow

School Manners

- Be on time; other students are waiting, and it is not fair for them to have to be interrupted or to waste their time catching you up when you do show up. Time is money!
- Clean up after yourself. Teachers are busy people, and it can reflect on your grade.
- Do your homework
- Do not skip classes
- Do not complain to others when it is actually your fault
- Only you are to blame! If you do not follow the rules and complete the requirements on time.
- Do not talk when the teacher or speaker is talking
- Do your homework
- Many smaller schools do not have custodians.
- Remember, you are a guest in the school, and there are many students, not just you.
- Speak to the teacher, not your neighbor, if you do not understand something Work Manners.
- Be on time. People are counting on you.
- Clean up after yourself.
- Do not gossip

- Have Good (Excellent) workmanship
- Honesty
- Leave personal issues at home!

- **Remember who pays your cheque…no, it is the customer! Sometimes, imagine you are the boss. How would you feel?**

- Take your vacation or holiday days as assigned; sick days or other missed day requests will cause stress to someone else.
- Teamwork
- Use an agenda to write or type in all the important things needed for each day
- Wages are usually set to society's standards, your abilities, or the economy. For example, the employer has to pay more than your wage; if you are paid $10.00/hour, it costs the employer about $12.00/hour to have you.
- Work at work
- You were employed to make your boss's life easier. Here are some miscellaneous ones:

- Always return anything used in the same place and condition; ASAP and never lend it out while you borrow it.
- Ask a child before assuming
- Be careful where you wear perfume or cologne (allergies). Bring all that is required of you to whatever you are going to be doing
- Be honest
- Be kind
- Be on time
- Brush your teeth at least twice a day (check your breath during the day)
- Bring dry clothes if you are going swimming, especially in winter
- Check the weather before you fly
- Check your fire and smoke detectors twice a year (time change of spring and fall)
- Close your drapes at night
- Clean the house weekly; vacuum, bathrooms, and dusting
- Clean up and pick up after yourself daily
- Cross the road at the crosswalk
- Courtesy
- Cover your roses for the winter

- Cover up in the sun
- Dress appropriately
- Dispose of unused paint, hair dye, medication, ink, computer parts, or garbage in the appropriate place
(remember, we drink that water)
  Do not expect that everyone can see, feel, hear, smell, taste, think, or can be as fast as you
- Do not expect that everyone knows what you know
- Do not steal. The other person needs it also
- Do something nice or give a gift without expectations or strings attached. Do your share of the housework or chores. Give a child a few moments' notice/warning before he/ she has to leave, eat, bathe, or get ready for bed
- Do not buy anything on credit you cannot afford later
- Drive defensively
- Do not phone, drop by unannounced, or make noise
•Monday – Friday before 9:00 am or after 9:00 pm
•Saturday before 10:00 am or after 9:00 -11:00 pm (Friday also)
•Sunday before 10:00 -11:00 am or after 9:00 pm
- Floss your teeth once a day
- For good service, leave a tip of 10%-15% for hair hairdresser, server, taxi cab, day spa services, and paper person (BUT one should never be expected).
- Front yards should always be tidy, and lawns mowed
- Go to your Medical Doctor at least every five years for a check-up (more often as you get older, usually every two years)
- Give to a charity of your choice 10% in total of time or money (each month or yearly)
- Give up your seat to an elderly or pregnant woman
- Give to goodwill
- Hang out with people who are like you and make you feelgood
- Have special toys put away when company comes if a child does not like to share
- If you are cold, wear warmer clothes
- In North America, look at someone's eyes when talking to them
- In some countries, do not throw toilet paper in the toilet
- Keep legs together when wearing a dress or skirt
- Ladies go first

- Look both ways before crossing the road
- Many children can hear and remember from at least the age of two
- Many power tools need education before using them
- Make notes or call yourself and leave a message to remind yourself
- Make your bed every morning

Mind your manners

Only tell a child or person what they are asking, not an hour of detail

- Own up to your own mistakes
- Pay for what you break
- Pay your bills on time
- Pay your taxes on time and in full
- Pick up after your animals
- Put away anything that holds water when it freezes, or use a pipe warmer
- Proper use of language
- Respect and follow the law
- Read and follow the rules and regulation signs
- Read the fine print
- Recycle and remember when recycle day is and put into proper bins
- Remember you are a guest anywhere but at your own home
- Remove the weeds from your yard. Feng Shui energy is better when people driving by think well of you!
- Ride your bike with a helmet
- Save a little money for a rainy day (three to six months savings is suggested)
- Say, excuse me when you have burped, farted, hiccupped, or sneezed
- Say 'Please and Thank you'
- Sit properly
- Share equally
- Shoes, shirts, and pants are required in most restaurants for health reasons
- Smile
- Split food and drinks up instead of giving to a child to share
- Spring clean yearly; wash windows, wash walls, move furniture, and vacuum under it

- Take a bath or shower (norm, every other day)
- Take the garbage out (at the very least, weekly)
- The engagement ring should be worth three months' salary (but ask your partner what they are expecting)
- Think ahead
- Visit the sick
- Walk, do not run when going around a pool
- **Wash your clothes after wearing them once**

Watch underarm smell, use deodorant when needed

- Wash dishes daily
- Wash your hands
- Watch and listen to body language –know when to be quiet or to leave
- Wear a bathing suit to public beaches
- When it hurts…stop
- When playing cards, wait until everyone has their cards before you pick up your hand
- When someone asks how you are doing, do not go into detail unless they ask
- While in a washroom, throw away the paper or toilet paper that fell on the floor
- Write important dates on a calendar and keep the calendar where you can see it
- Use a parachute when jumping out of a plane

**How many do you do?** _____
80% to 100% is great. If you need anything else, you better start learning some new ones.

These are the ones that will get you into trouble
Check off what you do but should not do:

Do Not
- Assume
- Believe everything you hear
- Believe that you have to always say yes. Believe that you have to listen to telemarketers, door-to-door salespeople
- Be loud in a public place
- Force a child to eat everything on their plate
- Believe that a customer is always correct (but do listen first and try to fi x the problem)

Fairy Tales, Dreams and Reality...

- Cheat
- Dive into water until you know how deep it is
- Drink and drive
- Drive without a license or insurance
- Eat poison
- Eat the last item without offering it to others first
- Expect everything at your beck and call
- Gamble your food or monthly bills money
- Get in a vehicle with someone you do not know

Graffiti anything that does not belong to you

Interrupt a conversation

- Judge others
- Keep food in the tent when camping
- Leave a child unattended
- Make inappropriate sounds or say anything rude
- Overstay your welcome
- Park in handicapped parking without a permit
- Pee in a pool or hot tub
- Place tongue on metal that is very cold or frozen
- Poke a sleeping dog
- Pour white gas onto a lit fire
- Speak your mind when nobody asked
- Smoke in bed, when really tired, or in a public place
- Spend more than you have
- Steal
- Stop a heavy-moving object
- Stick fingers in an electrical socket
- Take candy from a stranger
- Throw a ball in the house
- Touch a hot surface
- Touch fi re
- Touch or use anybody's tools or belongings without asking
- Throw away garbage or gum on the ground

If you do not like it…**then change it!**

The faster you do change the bad, the better your life will be.

Fairy Tales, Dreams and Reality...

## Change

Modification signifies the shift that transpires from one condition to another.

Magicians have given the perception of magic through materialization, vanishing, optical illusion, mind reading, and fantasy…changing a person's belief from a normal state to an unbelievable state, where they will second guess what they just witnessed for days. Check out Cris Angel's- Mindfreak show or even his website and see for yourself.

Hypnotherapy also has the gift of transformation; the mind is a powerful tool. I have witnessed a woman under a deep trance in hypnosis who was told she was as stiff as a steel bar and as strong as ten bars. The hypnotist then had a couple of men span her between two chairs, with just her neck and ankles touching the top edge of the chairs that were padded by a couple of jackets. The hypnotists then got up on a chair, climbed onto her stomach, and stood on her for a minute. She barely flinched from his weight, which was probably twice hers.

You can change anything in your life that you want to…all you have to do is believe! **Change reshapes energy…**

### Physical Change:
Throughout history, change has been defined by varying points of view.
 Past historical figures have also had a major impact on change and how we view the world, such as;
•     Ptolemaic astronomy envisioned a largely static universe, with erratic change confined to less worthy spheres.
•     Galileo tried to prove the Earth was round and spent his whole adult life in jail for his belief.
•     Isaac Newton and Gottfried Leibniz harnessed mathematical concepts into calculus to provide mathematical change models. This constituted a major step forward in understanding flux and variation. In modern physics, the concept of change is associated with action.
•     Thomas Alva Edison developed many devices that greatly influenced life around the world, including the phonograph, the motion picture camera, and a long-lasting, practical electric light bulb
•     The Wright brothers, Orville and Wilbur, were two Americans who invented and built the world's first successful airplane

- Elisha Gray, American inventor, invented and patented many electrical devices, including a facsimile transmission system
- Yuri A. Gagarin orbited the Earth in the spaceship Vostok I, which was launched on April 12, 1961, in a flight lasting one hour and forty-eight minutes.
- Alan Shepard Jr. was the first American in Space on May 5, 1961.
- The first man on the Moon and first step was by Neil Armstrong, and followed right behind him was Edwin "Buzz" Aldrin on July 20, 1969.
- 1981, Bill Gates and the Microsoft. Note he did not design the computer, just the software. IBM and many other companies invented and improved the computer. **Social Change:**
Cultural attitudes towards change:
- Change = Evolution

Change does create us to adapt. People generally do not like to change or have their environment change. It is not easy to change a culture, let alone a family member. *Changes in society have been observed over the years through slow, gradual modifications in mindsets and beliefs as well as through dramatic action (revolutions).*

History is the best tool used for this fact.

- Prehistorical periods
- Ice age
- Stone age
- Copper age
- Bronze age
- Iron age

- Ancient history
- Mesopotamia
- Old Kingdom
- Shang Dynasty
- Zhou Dynasty
- Roman & Greek empire

- Middle Ages
- Dark ages
- Medieval
- Viking

- Renaissance
- Modern era
- Industrial Revolution
- Machine Age
- Age of Oil
- World War I & II
- Atomic Age
- The Sixties
- Cold War
- Space Age

- Post-Modern
- Information Age
- The Seventies
- The Eighties
- The Nineties

- New Age
- The 21st century

Thought focused enthusiastically on transformation in management, in function and in mental attitudes, while ignoring or deploring changes in society or in geopolitics.

Many of us do not like to change and will fight it with tooth and nail for fear of the unknown. Change is the only real constant, for you can always count on it happening. You must embrace change and take it under your wing and learn to cope and understand that everything changes and will keep changing: age, beauty, friends, weather, water, plants, animals, buildings, currency, politicians, laws, and even; education, history and religion will change with enough time.

If you do not believe you can easily change… you can always dream about it!

**Conclusion:**

At this point of the book, you should have realized by now that you can have a great life. You deserve a great life, and all you have to do is start on a new path if you do not. Once you understand that you and you alone created your path and finally realize that you do not like the path…you can change it!

Throughout this book, I have written in many different ways about how to change your current path if you do not like it by the way of Fairy Tales, Dreams, and Reality. You have three different versions to help you understand that you can change your destiny and create a new path that will lead you to your deepest Wishes, Dreams, and Desires.

Remember, you only choose if the experience is good or bad.

**Your personal belief of your memories in the subconscious** creates your experiences and your path outcome. What you believe and how you respond when someone comments about your choices or dreams.

Remember, the only difference between a person who is eighteen and one who has just graduated is a person who is seventy facing a new life path, be it divorce, loss of job or spouse, or just wants something better in life, is that the teenager has nothing to lose and the older person is too scared to lose anything and take a chance on a new path.

In childhood, you are at your parent's mercy and have to do what they say legally until the lawful age of adulthood. You only get to make small decisions like who you hang out with at school and what you wear, eat, and play with. Remember that as a teenager, what you were allowed to do depended on what kind of parents you had, and most of the time, it would depend on what they did as a kid or what they believed was right. They are living and responding to you the only way they know how to.

As an adult, you know you are in control of your life and know that you are in control and living life as you believe you should be…Right?

Now, live your life! Be in control! Enjoy your dreams!

You have a mind of your own!

Remember, what you think is what you create, and your path is all because of you and only you!

**Again…Pleasure and Pain!** Do you like what you created?

*And if not, remember, every day is a new day to bring change into your live…*

*and create a new path that you do enjoy!*

Note from the Author;

**Tools for change:**
I have given many ideas for you to try and practice until you have the new path of your dreams.

Please permit yourself to live a *Fairy Tale* life and have wonderful *Dreams* to bring into your *Reality*. Once you are through reading this book, there are other great ideas to keep you on your new path, such as other books, movies, meditation, group counseling, spiritual groups, courses, or maybe travel to another country and view their way of life.

Keep on learning to expand your beliefs…

I have found that my fairy tales and dreams come true and become my reality… I did ask to live in a castle…which I did.

*I just forgot to ask to own it…and for how long.*

***Good Strength on your Journey!***
Love and Light, Connie

Fairy Tales, Dreams and Reality...

# APPENDICES

Bibliography

Information:

- Definitions sourced from Wikipedia.
- Information provided by Connie Brummet, owner of Canadian Institute of Natural Health and Healing.
- Brain & Limbic System photos purchased from Istockphoto.com.
- Front cover drawn by Jennifer Louie, Augustine Louie Design - Toronto, Ontario, Canada.

# EPILOGUE

I truly love to teach and share my knowledge with others. It makes me soooo happy when someone comes up to me and shares his/her experience of how
-my books or courses changed his/her life path.

Love and Light Connie

*Also Available*

Play the game Ikona and test
your Virtues and Sins

For additional information on

Constance Santego's wide range of Motivational Products,
Coaching Sessions, Spiritual Retreats,
Live Events and Educational Programs

Go to

www.ConstanceSantego.ca


Follow me on:

Instagram - Constance_Santego &
Facebook - constancesantegoo

YouTube Channel - Constance Santego
Subscribe and receive free information & meditations.

Dr. Constance Santego is a highly respected expert in the field of holistic health and spiritual healing. With over twenty years of experience teaching courses on these subjects, she has developed a deep understanding of the interconnectedness of the mind, body, and spirit in achieving overall well-being.

Dr. Santego holds a Ph.D. and Doctorate in Natural Medicine, which has provided her with a comprehensive understanding of alternative healing modalities and their application in promoting optimal health. Her educational background has equipped her with the knowledge to address health concerns holistically, considering the physical, emotional, and spiritual aspects of an individual's well-being.

Throughout her career, Dr. Santego has been committed to sharing her knowledge and empowering others to take control of their health and healing. She uniquely can blend scientific research and traditional wisdom, creating a bridge between conventional and alternative medicine.

In her "Secrets of a Healer" educational series, Dr. Santego draws upon her vast experience and expertise to captivate readers with her insights and teachings. She takes readers on a transformative journey, delving into the realms of holistic health, spirituality, and self-discovery. She aims to inspire individuals to tap into their innate healing abilities and embrace a balanced and harmonious approach to well-being through her writing.

Dr. Santego's work has touched the lives of many, guiding them toward a more profound understanding of themselves and their connection to the world around them. Her series is a beacon of wisdom, offering practical tools and techniques for personal growth and transformation.

Overall, Dr. Constance Santego's blend of knowledge, experience, and passion makes her a captivating figure in the field of holistic health and spiritual healing. Her contributions through teaching, writing, and her spellbinding series continue to inspire and empower individuals on their journeys toward well-being and self-discovery.

www.ingramcontent.com/pod-product-compliance
Lightning Source LLC
Chambersburg PA
CBHW071007120626
46546CB00003B/976